Heart First

Book #1

Heart First

A Female Psychedelic Call to Adventure

Michelle Miller

Preclaimer

Heart First is a personal memoir, wherein everything written *did* in fact happen. I've had to recall some instances to the best of my ability, especially dialogue, but nothing has been embellished. Everything I have included here accurately expresses the necessary information, feelings, or the mood of that particular time in space. Nearly all the names in the book have been changed to protect the guilty, or those who wish to remain anonymous.

*The statements in this book have not been evaluated by the Food and Drug Administration. The products and substances mentioned are not intended to diagnose, treat, cure or prevent any systemic dis-ease; *however,* those may be possible side effects experienced by the reader. That, and hopefully so much more!

Contents

Chapter 1

Mother Earth

As I sat in an old beat-up sedan with three complete strangers, it felt like one of those glowing, ah-ha, opera singing, psychedelic, everything-has-been-leading-me-to-exactly-this moments. I had been using mind altering substances for years, so getting into a car at an Alaskan music festival with these older hippies to trade my shwag weed (an undesirable substance as far as I was concerned) for their liquid LSD (my favorite psychedelic), was an incredible opportunity.

My life was lacking any direction, and that was a good thing! Instead of being herded along by societal pressures, I was free, flying by the seat of my pants while opening myself to limitless possibilities. Anything could happen, and it usually did. Guided by synchronicities, I'd follow signs, allowing my life to unfold organically, one momentous opportunity at a time. In fact, it was a full-time job being present enough to *actually notice* when opportunities such as this presented themselves.

Just then the long haired, bearded, bathing-in-patchouli man turned to me in the back seat, vial in hand and asked, "Where do you want me to pour it?" I had assumed they would have sugar cubes or paper to drip a few drops of this life-changing magic elixir on to, making this a to-go transaction. This was something I had thought to partake in as an enlightening recreational *daytime* activity at my leisure, but apparently, we were not on the same wavelength. When I told them I lacked any paraphernalia as well, his friend reframed the question, "Noooo, where would you like us to pour it; your eyes, your tongue, your hand?"

Instantly I understood, but I *really* hadn't planned on taking LSD that night. I had invited my best friend and tentmate Holding to go with me to their car, but it was past 10 p.m., and he had said he was tired. Our other two friends we were traveling with had already gone to bed, and Holding said he was headed back to our campsite shortly, too. An LSD trip lasts roughly six to eight hours, which is why it's called a trip at all because it feels like a short journey or voyage into an unfamiliar place (an altered state). Just like a great vacation, you usually return from a psychedelic trip somehow changed. At twenty years old, I was a seasoned journeyer, but this was not somewhere I had thought to go that night, especially all night long; alone, or surrounded by strangers who were not having the same experience.

I voiced my hesitation, but they insisted they wanted the weed. I considered walking away, just giving them enough pot to roll a joint or two, though now the opportunity to leave my body and expand my mind was knocking a bit louder, with more immediacy. As I sat amongst these older hippies, probably twenty years my senior, I also saw this as a chance to impress and gain acceptance as a worthy young member of the tribe. Without overthinking I answered, "hand," holding my left palm up over the center console.

As my new friend poured somewhere between five to seven drops (having *no* eye dropper inside the vial either) into the palm of my hand, his jaw fell open, as if in slow motion, which served as confirmation that he had accidentally over poured. We were all momentarily frozen, staring at the small puddle in my hand, acutely aware of its significance. One hit (or drop), which contains roughly 125 to 150 micrograms of lysergic acid diethylamide, would be the dosage for a "normal" trip most likely consisting of a major body high and some visuals. This, if ingested, would be an epic journey, my most epic to date. I contemplated pouring it back or shaking it off. Judging by the look on their faces, I don't think they would have blamed me. Besides, it was already in my hand long enough for me to feel some effects even if I poured the rest away. I offered to share, but everyone declined. As it often happened, my inner show-off rose to the occasion, and it was as if that facet of myself that delighted in shaking things up and shocking others involuntarily raised my hand to my face and had me quickly lick my palm, sucking all that sweet metallic liquid down. Now, there was a mixture of fear and amazement in the air as I quickly began to give them their weed. I knew the amount of time I could still function so-called normally was limited. Having smoked too much of that seedy brown weed all summer, I passed on sharing a joint with them, hurrying to get back to the music and find my travel buddy as soon as possible.

Spinning and laughing on an adrenaline rush spiked by my own astounding action, I happily made my way back across the lawn towards the outdoor stage. I returned to the section in the thinning crowd where I had left Holding, but he was nowhere to be found. I began to feel a tingling in my tongue and a lightness in my body, the telltale signs of the liquid acid coming on just as the band finished their last song, bidding everyone a good night. What!??? My friends were presumably asleep back at camp and the festival was over for the night? I was about to be high on the most heroic dose of LSD I had ever ingested and I was all by myself!

I knew I couldn't go to bed, so I set out to look for any signs of an after party. I wandered along the edge of the grassy field adjacent to the stage, exploring the fringe of the vendor area. I passed booth after empty booth until finally, I saw the familiar face of the handsome, long-haired crystal prism guy. Our eyes met as he looked up from packing his glass work away and we exchanged greetings and a smile. Then he yelled, "Hey, you're the marijuana girl!" I told him he could get more tomorrow, but he lurched out across the counter of his booth, his arm outstretched in an attempt to grab me. My instincts told me he didn't want more weed, that he wanted *me,* or he was unhappy with the quality of the marijuana we had sold him. I jumped to one side, dodging his arm and began to run. When I looked back, I was shocked to see he had made his way out from behind the booth and was now chasing me. I ran down the open field of the festival grounds as fast as I could. Before long, I looked back just as he seemed to realize the absurdity of what he was doing. He paused, with his hands on his thighs. He was bent over panting, and then shaking his head, he turned around, returning towards his booth. My heart was thumping, blood was flowing, and my mind began to step aside as my psychedelic journey began.

As I reached the edge of the forest, I finally slowed my pace. Entering the woods I saw the twilight sky, the tall mossy trees, and the forest floor all pulsating with life. Every natural thing had a rhythm that was emanating from it like white ripples into the ether, perfectly synchronized with my heavy breathing. As I inhaled, I received this white wave of energy that was radiating from the bark of the trees, the leaves, the moss and the Earth itself. As I exhaled, my breath hovered momentarily and then softly dispersed, losing itself within the matrix once again.

I began to see images of the Earth's intricacy as her many systems were simultaneously presented to me; garden rows of food she produces, trees that give us oxygen, passing clouds and flowing streams. I was shown our human bodies, with their complex systems; organs, muscles, fluids, and nerves which symbiotically allow us to process her oxygen, food, and water. I saw our reproduction systems and our ability to create life itself. The stages of our lives quickly passed before my eyes, from babies to children, middle aged to elderly, and finally our souls leaving our bodies and our physical remains returning to the Earth, becoming part of this very system. As these souls hovered above in the atmosphere, I realized that our spirits are eternal. My heart swelled with the knowledge of these miracles and then cracked with the awareness that the planet continues to take care of us, despite the incessant harm that we inflict upon her.

I then felt the Earth's pain. The pain humans have caused, placing material gain above all else. I saw that as a species we are losing our connection to nature, as well as our connection to our own true nature. We have put our faith not in the natural world, or in God, but instead worshipping money and status while allowing manmade systems such as the government or organized religion to be the ultimate truth. The fact that the government has taken the expansive, infinite nature of our spirits and boiled our identities down to a little photo and number on our ID cards became implausible to me.

I felt called to release myself from the entanglement of our tainted collective reality. I realized that whatever I chose to do in this lifetime, it had to be in harmony with the Earth and with my true nature. I needed to help the planet and others, not further harm them. I reached into my heavy hemp pants pocket and pulled out my colorful hippie wallet. As a pledge of allegiance to Mother Nature, I renounced everything that money stood for and rid myself of my government ID (the number they have branded and defined me with). Making a deep guttural sound, I threw my wallet and all of its contents into the forest. I watched the vibrant colors, as if in slow motion go somersaulting into the spruce trees, landing somewhere in the undergrowth. And then, things became even more intense.

As I looked around at my surroundings, the reality of the situation (as I understood it), came flooding in. People were chasing me, in the woods, in Alaska, and not only was winter on its way, the entire planet was dying! I knew I had to build a shelter if I was going to survive. I spent what I can only guess was an hour or two trying to move large logs in a teepee fashion that were mostly too heavy for me. I went through emotional peaks of planning, trying and then failing to move timber on my own. At one point I fell, landing on my stomach. Looking up, I saw Mother Nature herself, within a beautiful tree. Her face was the bark protruding from the trunk, framed with thick green leaves for hair.

Her arms were branches and her legs were roots which began to move outwards, spreading themselves longer, thinner and then eventually crumbling, dying, and returning to the earth. I began to see the destruction of the planet flash before my eyes in fast forward. Cities came crashing down and plants began enveloping the buildings, growing over them and swallowing them whole. Yellows and oranges flashed as fires burned and change continued, until finally a big red bang occurred, and we came full circle into absolute darkness and silence. Nothingness.

This was the last thing I remember before I would like to say I "fell asleep," but a more accurate description would be "passed out," face down in the moss, arms outstretched, exhausted from the emotional intensity of everything I had been through.

I awoke at about 4:00 a.m. to the sounds of trucks on the nearby highway. The first thought that crossed my mind was that I would be rescued by these trucks. They would save me from being alone in the forest and having to endure the Alaskan winter. I then began to realize how I had gotten there, that I was with friends, in the summertime, and that the Earth and I had both survived the experience. The next thing I noticed was that my flannelled arms were completely covered in mosquitos, including my bare wrists and hands. However, I had not one bite, which tells me (and scientists may want to research this) that the incredible amount of LSD I had pulsating through my veins may have doubled as a conscious expanding agent and as mosquito repellent.

I spent the next hour retracing my steps looking for *(yes)* my wallet because even though I *was* now fully committed to choosing the health of the planet over material gain, I did realize the necessity of having my ID. Shortly after 5:00 a.m., having been unsuccessful, I wandered back to camp absolutely drained. As I unzipped the tent, Holding asked me where I had been to which I could only briefly mumble something about the forest, LSD and losing my wallet. At a more reasonable hour, once everyone was awake, they were subject to the full version, Mother Earth and all, but mostly they were interested in how much money was in my wallet. "That is so *not* the point you guys! Don't you get it? I refuse to believe in a system whose underlying greed is destroying the planet!" And that was true, in fact, nearly everything I saw that night I interpreted as truth. In the days, months and years that would follow, this experience would continue to inform the person I was becoming.

As it often happens, no one took the girl on too much LSD very seriously. They just shook their heads in disapproval and Holding asked if he found my wallet, could he keep the money since it was of no importance to me. Sue's only response to my carrying on about Mother Earth was, "Miller, you should call your REAL mother."

Chapter 2

Experiential Learning

Though I loved my parents, I knew I would *not* be calling my *real* mother that morning. Neither one of my parents had ever experimented with psycho-active substances. Telling them I had thrown my wallet into the forest on LSD in renunciation of society was *not* something they could relate to. In fact, it would be cause for great concern on a number of levels. *All the levels.*

I came from the picture-perfect white middle class American family. My parents (still married) raised my younger sister and I in California, even though they are kindhearted mid-western Michiganders through and through. They did their best to instill their high standards of morality into us from a very young age. They taught us the value of education, hard work, and financial stability as well as the importance of community involvement and accountability in relationships with friends and family. They were also fun, playing games with us and never arguing with one another. By all accounts, they *should* have had two "normal" daughters, but I definitely didn't fall under that category, even at a very young age.

When I was eight years old, I'd start my mornings by rolling around on the floor whining and crying that I didn't want to go to school. This was the cumulative expression of not liking my teacher, a tumultuous relationship with my "best friend," and possibly low blood sugar, but the morning ritual was usually some variant of, "I CAN'T go to school," as I gasped for air while I sobbed. "I have nothing to wear . . . I'm hungry, and there is nothing to eat," I would continue whining, even though none of it was true. After days of suggestions as to what I could wear and what cereal to have for breakfast, my mother's patience began to run thin. She started tape recording these episodes to play, "when your father gets home." Though that *did* get my attention, I knew the third grade was *not* how I wanted to be spending my days. I was well aware that the possibility of Saturday activities such as sleeping in, watching cartoons, bike riding, and reading the books of my choice were simultaneously running in the background of any given school day, yet were unavailable to me.

My parents held traditional roles in my family. My mom was the caregiver, housekeeper, and cook. My dad was the breadwinner, garage tinkerer and disciplinarian. He was a chemist working for a company that manufactured ink for newspapers based out of Michigan where my sister and I were born, though he transferred to California when we were both young. Every morning, he would wake up at 5:30 a.m., dress in a suit and tie, and commute from our middle-class Southern Californian home to the City of Industry. Depending on traffic, he normally spent at least an hour and a half commuting each day. To talk with him now, he says he enjoyed his job, but growing up that wasn't what I perceived. I always remember him complaining about traffic and being very grumbly if we were too loud later at night because, as he would regularly remind us, "I have to get up very early for work in the morning." To me, he didn't seem happy with his job, and I wondered (sometimes aloud) why he did it all. "Because I have to put food on the table, Michelle. It's called responsibility." Hmmmm, to me that sounded more like an obligation than something he truly wanted to do. "Responsibility," my younger sister Amy would chime in, as if it were a spelling bee, proudly demonstrating her command of the word. "R-E-S-P-O-N-S-I-B-I-L-I-T-Y, responsibility. Can you even spell responsibility Michelle?"

"Uggghhhh," I'd respond in frustration to all of them because even though I was three years older, no, I could not. I didn't want to spell it, and I didn't want to have it. Not if responsibility meant doing something you felt *forced* to do.

My mother was highly involved in our lives when we were kids. She worked part-time at our elementary school and was the star volunteer in our classrooms. She stressed the importance of extra-curricular activities and encouraged us to stay busy playing sports or a musical instrument, joining clubs, and taking art classes. She was creative and always provided fun activities for my sister and I at home. I loved art and was interested in music, especially when I learned that music class was held during (and would possibly get me out of) fourth grade math. When I found out that I would need to make up the math homework in addition to practicing a musical instrument, I quickly decided music class wasn't for me.

Mom was also very domestic, which I began to see as a weakness. It seemed she did everything for us and my father and nothing for herself. When I saw her ironing my father's clothes and packing his bags for a business trip I asked, "Why can't he do that himself?" I didn't ask out of curiosity but straight up ten year old disapproval.

"I don't mind doing this for him," she said, trying to hide her visible annoyance under a fake, forced smile. "Your father works hard all day for us, so this is my way of supporting him and doing my part to contribute to the family."

"*Ironing* is your contribution?" I dug in deeper.

"That and cooking, cleaning, taking care of you girls. Maybe one day when you're married, you will understand." But that was a hard no. I didn't think I would ever find any satisfaction in ironing a man's clothes.

I was glad my parents were still married, as divorce was all around us in Southern California, but I vividly remember going to my best friend's house after school one day and watching her unlock their front door with a key she wore on a string around her neck. Her parents were divorced, and she lived with her mom who owned her own business and was often not home at night, but instead out with her boyfriend. I remember wishing I was a latch key kid like this and could open my own door to self-governed afternoons and complete homework freedom. She assured me her mom was very strict and would call her regularly to make sure she was getting her chores and homework done. But as we chose our own snacks and plopped down on her couch, turning on the television to whatever we wanted (something I wasn't allowed to do, especially not before I finished my homework), I realized this was a huge contrast to what I was beginning to view as my mother's overinvolvement in my life.

My grandma, or "Magic Grandma," as my mom called her because she would clean our glasses or dishes making them magically disappear back into the cupboard before we even finished our drinks, was the only one who I felt understood me. She was real magic to me. She was the first person to introduce me to the idea of an alternate plane of reality. Always light, happy, laughing and grateful, Grandma shared the details of how she could astral travel with me. She claimed her astral body (or her soul) would leave her body and float around the world, sometimes well directed by her, and other times in a dreamlike state. She described it as floating like a ghost high above Switzerland and other foreign lands. "But what do you do there, Grandma?" I asked.

"Oh, I just look in windows and at the people. I remember seeing one little girl playing inside her bedroom who looked up at me."

When I shared this with my parents, my father's comment, only half-jokingly was, "Bullshit, your grandmother says a lot of things."

Grandma told me to close my eyes, focus on my breath and imagine my third eye, as well as the image of two third eyes, one in each of the open palms of my hands. From there, I presumed I would get "beamed up." These were my first attempts at meditation, but in all honesty, I never saw any results from this. I also started attempting to move matter with my mind and my sister and I both talked about the energy we would see in tiny particles when we first turned off the lights at night. I called it the worms, and she called it the balls.

At 12 years old, I began questioning our household Sunday church-going belief system. I would travel down paths of open thought by asking simple questions like: "If God is love, why would *he* (this large man I envisioned who sat on a throne in the sky because he was the Holy Father) send anyone to burn in hell?" Information would always lead me to what I believed to be commonsensical conclusions such as *a **loving** God would **not** send billions of non-Christian people to burn in hell for an eternity.* I would share my findings with my mother, as this was a seriously alarming hypocrisy that seemed to undermine the world's largest religion's very foundation. She would admit (usually with a long sigh) that I did have a point, but that she didn't have any definitive answers. "Nobody really does," she would say. "I guess that's just where faith comes in."

But nope, that was not good enough for me when it came to *billions* of people, who in my mind, would unjustly burn in hell. I couldn't put my faith into this vengeful, supposedly loving God, the same way that I couldn't agree that there was only one systematic formula for living in the world. Something was telling me that there was more to life than going to college, having a career, getting married, buying a house and having a family (all in that order), but I didn't know what that more could be.

I began to wonder if there was a connection between what I noticed was going unanswered in Christianity and what was missing in my school text books. Both seemed to be glossing over completely horrendous acts: hell, holy wars, slavery and the decimation of Native Americans. I could see what I was being presented with at school was a very one-sided, candy-coated version of the whole truth that lacked compassion, much like this vengeful God. I empathized deeply with minorities, especially Native Americans, who had lived with such a reverence to the earth. It was unfathomable to me how they could be violently removed from their own land. My mother's response of acknowledgement, but not lingering on any of these topics seemed to echo the general population's sentiment. I felt as if I was uncovering a number of systemic problems that the rest of my world was willing to overlook and therefore, was somehow in compliance. I began refusing to go to church and started looking for other answers regarding creation, reality and our purpose here.

I was reading the Bible, exploring my own thoughts, and listening to music, which became a huge part of my life. I spent hours in my room dissecting lyrics that came through the radio, cassette tapes, and later, CDs. Classics like Buffalo Springfield confirmed for me that there was, "Something happening here, But what it is ain't exactly clear."[1] Big hair bands like Poison gave me "Something To Believe In," as they put these social hypocrisies to words such as religious embezzlement and the dichotomy between the rich and the poor.

At fourteen, while my mom volunteered as the high school PTA president, I sought out an alternative crowd that shared my growing distaste for rules and authority. My friends and I were the unruly West

---

[1] Buffalo Springfield, "For What It's Worth," single, Atco Records, 1966, vinyl

Lawn Kids who hung out on the hillside, west of campus apart from the jocks and cheerleaders, smoking weed and cigarettes and resisting mainstream culture. At fifteen I tried blotter LSD for the first time. My first few trips teetered on the precipice of mystically mind-blowing and totally immature. While at the beach, I experienced moments of expansive consciousness. I realized that one teeny, tiny, sparkly, golden grain of sand was part of thousands of grains beneath me and trillions upon infinite trillions of grains that stretched along this one particular beach, much less all the beaches and all the ocean floors on the entire planet!

I moved from this state of wonder to utter immaturity. My girlfriends and I would point at the people walking right by all the same sand, not noticing this obvious miracle. "Hello!" We shouted, "Don't you see all this sand? Aren't you noticing this? HelllllloooOOO!?" Laughing uncontrollably, we turned our back on these oblivious beachgoers and began to focus on the sea, having a similar realization about the water. The ocean was made up of infinite droplets of water, which, when put all together, are seemingly one. I then applied this Taoist-like philosophy toward myself. My physical body contains tiny, microscopic particles, just like the sand, little dots that make a whole. My whole is just one tiny dot in the entire universe, and I saw all of space is made up of these tiny dots of energy. I understood that there were infinite ways to move through space, connecting the dots which when put together, make up the connect-the-dot reality we choose for ourselves.

On the home and school front, my attitude was perceived as not caring about my grades and a conventional education. The general consensus was that I was smart, but I just wasn't "applying myself." This was true, and my failing multiple classes was evidence of that. But I was discovering many things (things I was actually interested in) by thinking for myself, or through observation, and now with the use of weed and psychedelics, the secrets of the universe had begun to unfold in front of me. It was no wonder why my flunking algebra (which everyone admitted I would probably never use later in life) seemed trivial to me. Adults were disappointed in *me* and my inability to get with the program, but I was disappointed in *them* and the program itself. I was frustrated by the lack of understanding about what I was experiencing, and aside from my psychology teacher who did encourage us to question (if a tree falls in a forest with no one around to hear it, does it make a sound?), I felt I only had my peers to look to for confirmation.

I began reprogramming and adopted the hippie counterculture mindset of my close stoner friends. I stopped trying to achieve what advertisers were determining was beautiful. Mainstream messaging (especially for women) was that our value lies solely in our outward appearance. I knew that was bullshit, that our value and qualities come from within. I became highly aware that this messaging was being presented to us by the very people who were selling this image of beauty, success, and happiness in the form of makeup, wrinkle creams, sports cars, big houses, vacation packages, and so on. We were completely bombarded with this superficial evangelism in magazines, newspapers and on the television, so I turned those outlets off completely. I quit caring about brand names, typically hiding my small frame under an oversized tie-dyed t-shirt and baggy men's shorts or a long flowing hippie skirt. I no longer spent time blow drying, hair spraying, and then curling my 80's style bangs perfectly up and over. A natural beauty, I gave up makeup completely and was now the girl with the hairy legs and armpits at my high school. My girlfriends and I became vegetarians to be more health conscious (as I smoked a pack of cigarettes a day), and as a statement against animal cruelty. We were into peace, love, creating art, cooking healthy food, bong hits and attending Grateful Dead shows.

Deadheads and their western gypsy caravanning provided me with evidence that something *could* in fact exist outside of the normal fabric of society. The parking lot of the Grateful Dead shows was a scene in and of itself. It was full of nomads who were living out of school buses and vans. There would be people holding up cardboard signs that read FREE HUGS, or I NEED A MIRACLE which referred to song lyrics, as well as the fact that they were in need of a free concert ticket. It was not uncommon for fans to bring extra tickets with the intention to gift "a miracle" to someone. Bartering and gifting was the preferred economy here, and all of this was magic to me.

These dirty, free-loving hippies were the first, and nearly only example I had as to what an alternative lifestyle that values people over profit could look like. They were stoking the small flame of imagination that I had already lit within me by showing me there was indeed another way to be in the world, aside from the conventional path I was being presented. All of this served as confirmation to what my friends and I were already discovering; that a good paying job, money, and material possessions were **not** necessarily going to fill our souls. But at sixteen all of this basically translated to, "Fuck the system," a system that was the only thing my parents knew. They began to turn up their volume, drilling me about my drug use, my lack of interest in school, and what they viewed as my uncertain future.

"Don't you want to go to college?"

"Are you even going to graduate from high school?"

"Don't you want a good paying job, a nice house, stability?"

It was the early 90's and the Reagan "Just Say No" (to drugs) campaign was still ringing in everyone's ears. It's zero tolerance policy left little room for conversation, and what I was being exposed to growing up in liberal California was unrelatable to my parent's sheltered Michigan upbringing. To their credit, they did want to know *why* I was using these substances and asked what they did for me, but these were extremely uncomfortable conversations with my dad on the front line asking most of the questions while my mom cried and listened. I tried to reassure them I was not going to fry my brain like an egg in a frying pan as the D.A.R.E. commercials demonstrated, but I lacked the maturity and vocabulary to describe these experiences. I didn't want to give them too many details, worrying them even more. I knew from my own firsthand experience that marijuana and psychedelics weren't dangerous in the way they were being portrayed in the media, but they weren't going to take their rebellious teenager's word for it. Not when mainstream media was telling them otherwise. Most of my friends weren't using harder drugs, and I knew cocaine, meth and heroin were entirely different beasts. My girlfriends and I were just having fun. We smoked weed on the regular, used psychedelics (mostly on the weekends), dabbled in huffing canned air, smoked coco-puffs (weed laced with cocaine which is different from snorting obviously) and a little nitric oxide (limited to Grateful Dead parking lots). "It's no big deal," was about the only comfort I offered my parents.

At school, I received the same line of questioning, especially from my older Spanish instructor. She was constantly slamming her ruler down on my desk saying, "Miller CÁLLETE," which was basically *shut up*. This would produce more giggles from the classroom than my disruptive behavior. I was failing her class, so she also began drilling me about my future. One particular day, all of this external pressure to get good grades and put more effort into the things I really had no interest in just to become a contributing member of the rat race came to a head. I remember my sarcastic response to her being that, "When I grow up, I want to be a bag lady." All the wrinkles on her face squished up in disapproval as I explained the benefits of being homeless as I understood them. As a bag lady I need not worry about a "real job." I could live for free, without bills and without worries or *responsibility*. "How will you eat?" she asked. To which I replied, "Dumpsters of course." Walking away, she shook her head, as if to say she was giving up and that there was no hope for me. I knew that homelessness wasn't *exactly* what I was aspiring towards. This remark was partly just to get my teacher off my back, but I also knew there was a certain truth hidden in my bag lady statement; that less was somehow more. I didn't want, nor would I ever need a big house, a white picket fence, lots of money or status. I saw at very best, these things were providing the adults around me with a sense of *satisfaction* or *security*, but they all lacked the blissful shine of the hippie community I had now encountered. I didn't really know what else there was, besides the American dream, so I landed on happiness. I would just start there, with the very basics. From then on, when anyone would ask me what I wanted to be when I grow up, I would answer, "Happy."

By some miracle, I did manage to graduate from high school in the Alta Loma class of 1994 with an overall grade point average of 2.4. I had absolutely no interest in going to college, but my parents forced me to apply. My mother was on the verge of a nervous breakdown due to my uncontrollable behavior. They would not allow me to stay under their roof just working, doing drugs, and partying with no foreseen direction in life. Remarkably, I was accepted to Chico State University, and only CSU, and my parents insisted I go. With no job or any other viable options in sight, I had no choice but to do just that. In the fall they drove me eight hours north and dropped me off with my bicycle for transportation to live in the co-ed dorms.

During my first semester of college, I did really well socially and was very disciplined, waking up early every morning to start my day with a pre-breakfast trail ride on my bike. I made friends quickly and loved exploring nature, concert going, and my new-found freedom, but other than the desire to be happy, I had no idea where I was headed, especially academically. I had no major, so in order to fulfill the general education requirements, I tried to take classes that interested me; eastern religions, english, critical thinking, communications, but I struggled. The schoolwork was hard, but the prospect of sitting behind a desk for four years and applying myself to something that really didn't serve a purpose for me was even harder. I knew a college education was a huge opportunity that I would be throwing away if I didn't continue, but it just seemed pointless. Everyone else viewed this institution as a path to upward mobility, but for me, it was confining, suffocating, and even oppressive. If I stayed in school, it would be mainly to please my parents, but most likely at the cost of losing my soul. There was a whole wide world out there that I was eager to travel and explore, but the only "safe" way to do so that was being presented to me was a semester abroad by maybe my third or fourth year in college. My flame that had been ignited would be inevitably dimmed by then, but I trudged forward.

When the second semester started, I hoped my new classes would bring more inspiration and a different perspective. I was most excited about my mixed media art class. I had a vision for the first assignment, which we were told at the end of class would be "A Portrayal of Opposites." My creative juices began flowing. I wanted to take a black boxy television set and adorn the top of it with greenery, natural materials, and some of my crystals, comparing the manmade artificial world with the beauty of the natural world. However, I discovered during the second class session that we were to *draw* the assignment, and the mixed media element was either paint, charcoal or pastels. *Fucking A!*

That night in my dorm room, I attempted to sketch my idea a number of times, but as a drawing, it just wasn't the same. The limitations in what was to be my only fun class amplified my entire experience in the world at large and before I knew it, I was crying uncontrollably with a stream of frustrations running through my mind. *I can't even express myself creatively the way I want to in **art** class! The system lacks any imagination at all! I'll be penalized for creating something* *above and beyond the instructions that were given. I will have to conform if I want to get a grade. This is **all** bullshit, and I'm done!*

There was just no way for me to swallow the conformity pill. I had tried. Being there, with my parents paying an exorbitant price for this "experience" was only perpetuating the problem by funding a system I didn't believe in. I wanted to be part of the solution, or in the very least, find another way to live my life more creatively. I had no idea what that could look like, or what else could possibly materialize for me outside of the confines of social norms, but I had to step out and try to see. I wanted to think for myself.

Still crying, I angrily flipped through the pages of the student handbook in my dorm room, searching for the administration office's phone number. I pounded the seven digits in to inform them I would be dropping out of school. "You would like to withdraw?" came from the calm woman's voice on the other side. "Yes, I would like to withdraw," I responded, with a newfound sense of clarity and maturity, having used this more professional terminology. An incredible weight was beginning to lift.

The next day, after having signed all the paperwork and finalizing everything, I called my parents to let them know. They hardly seemed shocked, in fact, my mom was unusually calm given the magnitude of the situation. She quickly offered up some options, as if they had been preparing for this moment all along. First, she approved the check for the tuition being refunded to me, and I swore up and down that I wouldn't spend the money. Then, she gave me two weeks. In two weeks' time, she would drive to Chico, California to either help me move (if I had found a job and a new place to live), or to pick me up and take me back home to live once again under their roof, according to their curfew and following their rules. The latter was not an option. I set to work immediately applying to any and all minimum wage jobs.

As those next two weeks unfolded, I began to witness some sort of magic making its way into my life because as one of my greatest teachers Bob Marley sang, "When one door is closed, many more is open."[2]

---

[2] Bob Marley, "Coming In From The Cold," track #1 on Uprising, Island Records, 1980, vinyl

Chapter 3

Leaving the Ordinary World

My determination to stay in Chico landed me two menial part time jobs and a screamin' deal, subletting a three-bedroom apartment from someone who was in jail for just $275 a month. I promptly had an unsolicited candidate for a roommate, which I hadn't even considered. My friend Dan moved into the second room, and his drum set moved into the third. Dan was going to stay in school but preferred to *not* live in the dorms. So there we had it. Things had worked out for me quite quickly.

Proud of my accomplishments, I called my parents to let them know they need not move me back home. My father expressed his concern about having a guy for a roommate, which for him, was probably worse than dropping out of school. This had never even occurred to me. I ended our conversation by brushing him off knowing his concerns about Dan (he went so far as to tell me he didn't want me to end up pregnant) were completely unfounded. What was done, was done, and I tried not to let my dad's reaction tarnish the satisfaction I was feeling for everything I had managed to accomplish on my own. I was looking forward to daily drum sessions and weekend jams at our new place.

My mom insisted she would drive up to help get me settled in, even though I told her I was already settled. Our good friend Matthew Holding had helped Dan and I completely move out of the dorms and transport two new mattresses with his truck. We slept in our own rooms with mattresses on the floor and cooked with Dan's camping pots and pans. *What else did we possibly need?* During the days, he was off at school, and I was starting my new jobs. At night, we would smoke pot and cook dinner together. He would play the drums, and I enjoyed hosting gatherings with friends. My mom came up and witnessed all of this, and though I was embarrassed (but my friends loved it), she treated us all to pizza at the apartment. She bought Dan and I the kitchenware and dishes she deemed necessary as well as a table and chairs that *did* end up coming in handy.

I started splitting my free time between the friends I had made at school and amongst the older hippie community. The latter were professional tie-dyers, organic gardeners, drug dealers and festival organizers. They began to take me under their wings and teach me about sweat lodges, earth-based chants, gardening, natural remedies, the healing properties of herbs (mainly marijuana) and stones. This was Hippie 101, my dream class that had not been available at CSU.

I felt the same way about relationships as I did about my future; non-committal. I was happy and open to everyone I would meet, which often times my friendly energy would be misinterpreted as flirtation. I was receiving a lot of attention from older men (in their 30's, 40's and even 50's) for the first time in my life. For the most part, I didn't like the attention. I was interested in their knowledge and their alternative lifestyles, *not* in a relationship. I would help these older friends organize parties, set up festival booths, and volunteer at their organic farms. Aside from Matthew, or "Holding", as we would call him, I really wasn't interested in anyone. In fact, I really wasn't very interested in sex at all.

My first sexual experience had been when I was fourteen years old. I had slept with my friend's seventeen-year-old boyfriend who I was completely infatuated with. Or, rather, he had slept with me, because he was holding my wrists down the entire time, in my childhood bed. Though I wasn't fighting back, he had used his good looks, experience, and physical strength to initiate this sexual encounter, which he was entirely in control of. At one point, probably when he saw tears in my eyes, he asked if I wanted him to stop. I shook my head no, not wanting to be a tease and just wanting to get it over with. This was a manipulative form of date rape where my innocence and infatuation were used to add another check mark to this gorgeous guy's list of girls he had devirginized.

I felt like this experience had given me special 3D glasses to see *every* man's true intention, which was *sex*. In addition to not wanting to be valued for my appearance, I also didn't want to be desired solely for it either. This was another big reason I began to hide my body by dressing in oversized clothing to consciously deflect unwanted male attention. On a certain level, I knew that experience was serving to protect me. Though I had had sex on a small number of occasions since that incident, I wasn't promiscuous. This is how I knew I was *not* going to get pregnant or an STD. If I was going to have sex again, it was going to be with someone special, and the only person I was really interested in at that time was Holding. I found him adorable with his small, strong, tan frame. He had shaggy short hair, a thin beard and blue eyes underneath the John Lennon glasses that he wore. He was also a musician and had been spending a ton of time at our apartment, either playing drums or guitar with Dan or spending hours talking with me in my room. He knew my sexual history, and we would sometimes lay together in my bed, fully clothed, resting our heads on one another, just listening to music, talking, smoking cigarettes, and being infatuated with each other.

I was never an alcohol drinker. I preferred to smoke weed and would be stoned to the bone riding my bike to work, along the river, or down long stretches of quiet farm roads. I would blissfully peddle past rows and rows of orchards. *This* was my higher education and why I believe it's called getting high at all. I was escaping the ordinary, living on a higher plane of consciousness and experiencing the pure joy of being alive, wild, and free while connected to source and singing my heart out to songs like, "Wake up to find out that you are the eyes of the world.... wake now discover that you are the song that the morning brings..."[3]

By freeing myself from the clutter of all the ordinary things everyone else thought I *should* be doing, I had created more space for the extraordinary to appear in my life. I would think of a friend, hoping to meet them that day, and then take my time leaving the apartment, feeling lazy and honoring that. Riding my bike, I'd stop and sit by the river, have a smoke, and eventually meander on. Feeling like there was no particular place I had to be, I'd wander into whatever coffee shop I felt drawn to where I would see the exact same person I had wanted to meet with that day!

When yoga came on my radar, I took a random detour on my bike and stumbled upon a free yoga class in the park where I was invited to join. After a conversation with a friend, he told me I should read *Black Elk Speaks*, and later that day, while stoned, and casually eying another friend's bookshelf, I saw the book there. When I picked it up, he offered it to me as a gift.

As I began to witness everything in my life elaborately working itself out for me, I was beyond happy. I was radiating pure joy. I knew I was definitely waking up to discover *something*, but at that time, I really didn't know what that something was. This was before the Internet, spiritual quotes on Instagram or *The Secret*. I had never heard the word "woke" or awakening and had no idea if these coincidences were from above or from within me. I was both excited and perplexed wondering

---

[3] Grateful Dead "Eyes Of The World", track #6 on *Wake of the Flood*, Grateful Dead Records, 1973, Vinyl.

if this was as the Bible states, "ask and you shall receive." Aside from "you're manifesting," none of my friends could really explain how or why it was done, but I liked it. I was beginning to see that the Universe was conspiring *with* me to bring whatever I was calling into my life, even outside of my Chico bubble.

When a group of my college-going friends were planning a trip to San Francisco to see David Grisman in concert, I had a ride, but no money for a ticket. So, I actively began looking for another way to go to the show. Because David Grisman has composed music with Jerry Garcia of the Grateful Dead, he is an extremely popular folk musician within the hippie community and someone I really wanted to see perform. As I made my rounds on my bike to visit friends, I told anyone and everyone who would listen: "It's David Grisman's 50th birthday celebration!" I was casting my intention out into the matrix.

"Yeah, I know it's at the Warfield. I'm working that show," came the answer to my prayer from my long-haired professional tie-dye friend, Craig who was seventeen years my senior. "I can probably get you in. What's your last name?" he asked. "I'll put you on the list. Just ask for me at the front door." I was in! And I quickly let my friends know.

We parked Nikki's car downtown in a multi-level parking garage, and my group of friends got in line in front of the historic theatre preparing to enter with their tickets. I asked for Craig at the door, but that didn't pan out, and my name was not on "the list" either. As my friends waited for the doors to open, they suggested that one of them buy me a ticket and I pay them back later, but the small venue was sold out. I told them I would see them inside, but just in case, we made a plan to meet at Nikki's car after the show. I went to wander and was now holding my index finger up as I walked amongst the people standing in line, indicating that I was looking for a miracle ticket. Then, boom! Craig and I nearly walked right into one another. He had come out to smoke a cigarette and look for me, he explained as he led me around the back of the theatre. He said he thought he could get me in, but I would have to volunteer in the coat closet or something. I said that was fine as long as I could see the show, and he slipped back behind the heavy door to see what he could do.

After what seemed like a short eternity, a woman carrying a clipboard finally opened the backdoor. She took one look at eighteen year old me and stared annoyingly at the much older Craig whose face was right next to hers peering over her shoulder at the clipboard. She got to work explaining to me that I'd be helping with the coat check. She told me once everyone had seemingly gotten through the door, I was to come find her because she had another job for me. And like that, the second song in, once everyone's coats had been checked, I was dancing in the isle to "Panama Red" and "Midnight Moonlight." My task was then to man the VIP seating and not let anyone in without a ticket.

After the show I had to return people's coats, and then I went to find Craig to thank him. He was still busy but asked if I wanted to stay, adding, "There will probably be an after party." I knew this meant the possibility of meeting the band, but it would also mean staying the night with Craig, which I definitely wasn't interested in. Plus, my friends would be waiting and worried about me. We said our goodbyes, and I told him I'd see him back in Chico. When I got to the car, it was nearly two in the morning and everyone was gone. They had left a message with seven dollars and the keys rolled up inside a large sheet of lined notebook paper under the windshield wiper. *We got tired of waiting and left with Jen. We are staying at the Holiday Inn in Oakland, near the Airport. Here's money for parking.*

I drove down the circular parking structure, but the cost was over $20 and aside from what they had left me, I had no money at all. I turned the car around with the skeptical parking attendant watching and probably wondering the same thing that I was. What resources could possibly be awaiting me back on level two of the parking garage? With no one in sight, I decided to take a nap, feeling the cost of parking increasing with each breath. I figured if nothing else worked out, I could pan handle in the morning, or worst-case scenario, call my friends at the hotel from a payphone.

I slept until the sound of people talking and coughing woke me up. It was two younger business looking men who were clean cut, dressed in nice dress pants and shirts, ties loosened around their necks, and crouched down with their backs against the dirty white wall of the parking garage. As I left the car to approach them, I realized they were smoking something, which judging by the smell, I was not familiar with. I heard the word Angel in my mind. Maybe one's name was Angel because they looked to be Latin American. Maybe they were going to be my angels or possibly they were smoking angel dust. Whatever it was, they immediately offered it to me. "No thanks," I said politely. "Look, I was wondering if you could help me. My friends all left, and I'm stuck inside the parking garage without enough money to pay the bill to get out." Clearly drunk, in addition to whatever they were smoking, one replied, "Show us your tits," slurring as he fell back against the wall.

"Dude don't be an asshole. She needs help," the other interjected.

"I need money to get out of this parking garage."

"If you show me your tits, I'll help you out," he sputtered.

"I'm not going to show you my tits."

"How much do you need?" The nicer of the two asked.

"Twenty bucks."

"Give her twenty bucks," Mr. Nice Guy instructed his T & A friend who begrudgingly reached into his pocket, crumpled up a twenty-dollar bill and tossed it my way, muttering about how he had ruined *both* their chances to see my tits.

"Thank you," I chimed happily as I snatched the bill up from the ground. They offered me whatever they were smoking one more time, which I refused. I hopped in the car to consult the large paper map of the city guesstimating where the hotel by the Oakland Airport could be before making my way over the Bay Bridge right at daybreak. A number of other obstacles began to present themselves that morning as I was running out of gas and lost in what seemed like a very bad section of Oakland. But after a black man, who looked more confused by my situation than I was, gave me a quarter to use a payphone and warned me not to stop again in that neighborhood, I was able to call and eventually find the hotel around 9:00 a.m. I only managed to sleep for about half an hour on the hotel room floor before everyone was up, well rested, caffeinated and ready to head back to Chico. With my head propped up against the window in a state of grateful exhaustion, I gave thanks for having seen the show, my parking garage angels, finding my way back to my friends, and now home.

Despite repeated warnings from our landlady, Dan continued to play the drums, and we were now hosting large parties with live music on the weekends. On one of these nights, Erin, an older hippie admirer of mine, showed up and gifted me my own stash of liquid LSD as well as offered to dose our party guests free of charge for anyone interested. Sure! The fact that I was the underaged person (just eighteen years old) in charge and there were people spilling out of my apartment onto the asphalt parking lot never really crossed my mind.

I was mingling and smoking outside when I immediately *felt* Tucker's presence as he arrived. Tucker was neither a student nor a schmoozy old hippie. I had met him in a younger spiritual circle of drummers and yogis. We had only had one previous conversation, but I remembered it was about meditation. Like magnets, we gravitated toward one another, clearly in the same head space. I thought maybe *he* could explain the innerworkings to all the auspicious coincidences I had been experiencing. I was beginning to feel the LSD coming on and suggested we go on a walk. I greeted more friends arriving, orienting them towards the alcohol and LSD and then we excused ourselves, walking into the darkness out along the railroad tracks.

I started with small talk and said, "I haven't seen you for a while."

"Yeah, I was gone for about a month."

Our chatter slowed as we sat on the train tracks, and it was as if we were beginning to communicate information without words. I went from Tucker looking into my almond shaped eyes to my spirit lifting right out of my body, rising into a soup-like dark space sprinkled with pinpoints of lights. Our translucent, greenish souls began to float straight up together, dancing and twirling amongst the stars. I was transmitting my questions to him about these synchronicities and my ability to manifest, and felt like my entire being was absorbing the answers. "It's because you are light… living from your heart… pure intentions… because you believe… you are open to receive… you are grateful... grateful heart…. you are actually noticing," all emanated from him. Our souls stayed there pulsating for some time, but the answer to all of my questions seemed to come back to one thing. Love. A loving openness.

I don't know how much time passed, but in a snap we were back on the railroad tracks, sitting side by side as voices of people were approaching. I noticed that I was holding a cigarette and my lighter in my hand, which I hadn't been aware of before. I realized that during the entire experience I had probably been fidgeting with my lighter, and my hand was repeatedly attempting to light my cigarette nervously flick, flick, flicking. Tucker helped me to light my cigarette saying I shouldn't be smoking, and I heard his voice for the first time in what seemed like a very long time. I felt weightless and drawn to leave my body yet again but was worried about our safety with people walking towards us. He reassured me I needn't worry, and that I could trust that the Universe would always send me a sign if I was in danger. He confirmed, "They are still a long ways off," and we sailed toward the stars once again. This time instead of exchanging information, we merged, radiating pure energetic love and understanding into one another in the form of white light.

As the people became closer, we landed back into our physical bodies again. Assuming they would know we were leaving our bodies tripping on acid, I asked what we should do to appear normal. Tucker chuckled as he responded, "Talk. Talk about anything." He began to ask me how my job was, and I blabbed on, informing him it was *two* jobs. I started mumbling the words, "Work, work, work and today was sunny with some clouds in the sky." We laughed at the ridiculousness of going from hearts soaring to talking about the weather, verbalizing that this is a perfect example of how much surface level information we all communicate on a regular basis.

After the couple passed, I asked him how many hits of acid he had taken and Tucker's green eyes sparkled with his reply, "I'm not on acid. I just came from a thirty day silent meditation retreat." Not knowing *that's* where he had gone, I felt chills down my spine and new questions came flooding in. After thirty days of silence at an ashram, Tucker seemed to be on exactly the same LSD induced wavelength that I was on … or was he? Did he have the same visual experience that I had? I'm pretty sure Tucker would tell a different story. He probably just watched me flick my lighter for three minutes because when I asked if he felt like he left his body too, he just shook his head insinuating no and said he was wondering what I was on since I had really *high energy*. He said I was rambling on about the crossroads of my life. Hmmmm, we were obviously in parallel universes.

"Ok, live in love, but WHERE Tucker?" I asked. The lease on our apartment would be up come summer and as I saw it, I had two clear choices. I could be a full time *Spinner Girl* dancing on Grateful Dead tour or backpack up to Alaska to clean fish. Now it was Tucker's turn to be shocked, knowing I was a vegetarian. "Clean fish! How could you do that?" His suggestions for my immediate future were more personally fulfilling such as spending time at an ashram, within a spiritual community, or volunteering on an organic farm, *not* working on some kind of factory line slaughtering helpless animals.

As outlandish as this was, my life was already moving quickly in the fish killing direction even though yes, I was still a vegetarian. I had been talking to my close high school girlfriend Eva, who had worked there the previous summer. She had been filling me in on the details, and our plans were beginning to come together. This would be a good push for me. It was less about fish, and more about exploring new horizons, living closer to nature, and making some quick cash. This was the "trimming" (of marijuana today) of the 80's and 90's; working sixteen to eighteen hours per day. It was long, tedious work that paid minimum wage, but with lots of overtime, and there was nowhere or no time to spend your money.

Both Holding and my older suitors in the hippie community would have been happy if I stayed in Chico that summer. Grateful

Dead tour seemed the likely choice amongst my college friends, or Phish for that matter, but all of that seemed like it would be a rerun. I knew and loved these things, but they were predictable. I felt like I had somehow already received the necessary information from those experiences. I was ready for something new, something *next level,* and backpacking to rugged Alaska happened to be what had presented itself.

Chapter 4

The Egg Men

I set off for Alaska on a one-way ticket with my backpack, $300, and an ounce of good weed. I had no job prospects. In fact, it was worse than that. I had received rejection letters from all the fish canneries on the entire island. But I had been the driving force who convinced my three other girlfriends to do this with me, so I was determined to go regardless. The girls were skeptical. Each of them had secured jobs and were asking what my plan was which other than, "Just go and see," I really didn't have one.

I had spent my last week in Chico visiting with my Southern California friend Jana as we prepared for our Alaskan departure. During the day, I was obsessively cleaning my apartment in hopes to find the acid Erin had put on a piece of paper for me the night of my OBE (out of body experience). At night, Jana and I were hitting up the end of the year parties, and I was spending as much time as I could with Holding before we left. At one of these parties, Holding introduced me to Shane (a guy he had been telling me about who would also be spending his summer in Alaska). I was surprised Holding would introduce me to someone this good looking. Shane was a gorgeous flannel wearing sophomore with long blonde hair and a well-groomed goatee. When I asked him where in Alaska he was going, he told me to Petersburg, a tiny town with a population of 2,000 on Mitkof Island in the middle of fucking nowhere which was the exact same place we were headed! This was my planless confirmation cherry on top! What I was coming to realize about these coincidences was that they were messages that I was heading in the right direction. Shane told me he would be working construction off the grid all summer, but we discussed the possibility of returning to California together on an Alaskan ferryboat and then by land. This would be a cheaper and more scenic mode of transportation.

Jana and I were buzzing with excitement as our flight followed a perpetual sunset north. We met up with our other So Cal girlfriend, Eva during our layover in Juneau and then continued on to Petersburg together. Eva's older brother Big B (for Big Brother) and his friend Russell, who we all knew from home, picked us up at the airport ...*walking*. I thought they were joking as we retrieved our backpacks from the one room, one carousel airport. We stepped outside into what would be the equivalent of winter air for me, though it was late June. The nighttime sky was brighter than when we were flying over Washington State hours ago. I took in the panoramic mountain views as the boys reassured us that it wasn't far. Besides, taxis were rare and very expensive. As we walked, they filled us in on the local news and pointed out essential businesses and places. The salmon season was off to a slow start that year, and hardly anyone was working yet. Big B showed us the entrance to Tent City where I would most likely end up staying at some point this trip because I hadn't secured a job, and therefore had no employee housing. We saw the main grocery store, the post office, the library, and their favorite bar at the harbor side pizzeria. Lastly, he explained where the canneries were, sitting on moorings near the scenic harbor full of fishing boats.

We were here. Downtown Petersburg. Months of anticipation and it seemed we had seen the entire town in a matter of ten minutes walking. The boys said we still had to see The Boardwalk and The Stump Bar. They would come by to get us some time the following day. With that, we were left to our own devices and Eva, our guide and cannery veteran, set to work on negotiating my paying to stay with them at their cannery bunkhouse for a few nights. We tried to go about it the right way, but when we received a hard no from the receptionist, we had no choice but to take matters into our own hands. The girls snuck me in through the side door and let me stay in an empty bunk, temporarily saving me from Tent City. This was a village of sorts where the seasonal factory workers lived inexpensively by camping, but I was told I should only stay there as a last resort. I trusted that information.

In my mind, The Boardwalk would most likely be Petersburg's main attraction. As quaint as the fishing harbor was, I had pictured more. I imagined The Boardwalk to be similar to the Huntington Beach Pier, sprinkled with gifts shops and an ice cream stand at the very end. The next day, when we walked down a gravel road away from the ocean, I began to suspect this was not a pier but a different kind of tourist attraction all together. I must have looked very confused when we turned once again and began to walk deeper into the forest. The boys burst out laughing. "Here we are. See... a *boarrrddd-walk.*" They pointed to the trail made from elevated wooden planks that served to keep hikers out of the wet marsh or the infamous *muskeg* I'd been hearing about. They held their sides laughing as I described the double scoop waffle cone ice cream I had thought we'd all be eating and the souvenirs I had imagined would be available. I too laughed at the ridiculousness of my California expectations, and the further we walked, the more real the forest seemed to become. The boys pointed out the blueberry bushes that were nearly ripe on either side of the walkway. I noticed the colorful splash of wildflowers along the lush, mossy hillside. Before long, we arrived at a beautiful waterfall. In silence, we branched out, each of us enjoying the scenery in our own way; sitting, touching, listening to and watching the waterfall. I lit up a bowl, quietly sharing with Big B's friend Russell. It was here, in the serenity of this natural beauty, that I began to realize just how far I was from the hustle, bustle and even the irony of calling it the "real world." I began settling into this slower, more natural environment.

As we walked on towards The Stump Bar, I pestered the boys like a little sister for the third time. Now nineteen, I reminded them that unlike Eva and Jana, I didn't have the fake ID that was probably required to get into the bar. "I'm not much of a drinker anyway," I chattered on, stoned. "I'd rather smoke pot, but if everyone is going in, it will suck if I have to wait outside." They reassured me that it wouldn't matter here, I would be able to get in, but again they didn't provide any explanation for *why* they'd let me in. My mind spun off into a hopeful daydream where the boys were friends with the cute bartenders who would let me in, and The Stump Bar would become our regular hangout. As we made our way off the gravel road into a clearing in the spruce trees, I began to see a *literal* pattern here. The short stumps and logs that sat upright were in an unorganized circle which served as stools, bar stools. Again, the boys were in stitches, explaining that the locals, mostly teens, came here to hang out and drink in the woods. They also pointed out that the area was littered with gun shells and shot up aluminum cans from their target practice. This was the local entertainment. Why they thought this would even be a point of interest to us, I don't know. *My* Southern California teen activities had consisted of going to the mall, the movie theater or smoking clove cigarettes at pretentious cafes. Here, they combined underaged drinking and shooting guns. Got it.

Over the course of the next few days, I spent a lot of time on my own. I explored Petersburg and went into each of the fish canneries inquiring about work. While walking the streets, the ratio of women-to-men became extremely noticeable. I started counting; three men coming out of Kito's Cave, two smoking in front of the mini market, six, seven... I reached fifteen men, and then little old me. The rumor was it was thirty to one! Dressed in my usual thrift store wardrobe of baggy men's shorts that I now had over waffled long underwear, I wasn't exactly presenting as sexy, but I still had doors opened for me, received extra attention and the transient question of, "Where are you from?"

A third girlfriend, Cami had arrived, and now all of the girls were complaining that with hardly any salmon they had no work. They were locked into their company contracts acquiring debt from their housing and cafeteria bills. They now *owed* the fishing cannery money that would come out of their eventual paychecks. The irony of this was not lost on me. My not having so-called secure work was clearly providing greater opportunity and flexibility here. Granted, I was now living in Tent City because I had to vacate Cami's bed, but it wasn't that bad. It was a lot like the boardwalk. In order to elevate everyone out of the marsh, there were a series of wooden planks that connected "tent pads" or decks, where four tents could be pitched per deck. The wooden trails all led back to the main entrance and the community kitchen. I had at least one job prospect, which would hopefully lead to stay in a bunk house, and there was always my plan B. Eva had told me that weed was very expensive and hard to come by in Petersburg. For that reason, I had come prepared with my own supply and was willing to sell some as a last resort if it meant a plane or ferry ticket back to the "lower forty-eight" as they called it, meaning the lower forty-eight states.

In less than a week, I had landed myself a job in the Egg Room (which I knew nothing about) at Western Seafoods Company. At the pizzeria that night, I was excited to share my good fortune, but instead of receiving the congratulations I expected, I mostly received warnings. The consensus from the seasoned cannery workers was that the Japanese men that ran the Egg (or caviar) Room were horribly sexist, and though it wasn't hard work, it was extremely repetitive. Each person at this round table discussion had something to say.

"They make you pick tapeworms out of salmon eggs for eighteen hours a day!"

"You'll probably get tweezer fingers, but that *is* better than the carpal tunnel they get working on the fish production line."

"If you're lucky you'll get promoted to the rubbing tables working the mucous membranes of the egg sacks back and forth over framed chicken wire."

Hmmm, I thought, *this is turning out to be a great Alaskan adventure indeed!*

I was still half asleep when my 5:30 a.m. alarm sounded, and I found myself filing into the long line for the yellow school bus that would take us from Tent City to the cannery. I assumed these would be my co-workers, but as the newest face, they quickly did an assessment and began to set me straight. I was the only egg person, which was an "easy job" they informed me. Everyone within earshot began to gang up on me, teasing and reassuring me that the work I was about to do was nothing compared to the slime line where they worked actually gutting the fish. Feeling like I could cry, I shrugged it off saying I had no idea since it was my first day. Their energy changed as the bus arrived at the cannery. They empathized, pointed me in the direction of the egg department, and dispersed everyone going their own way.

I entered through the egg locker room, where someone offered me the white apron of a man who had recently left, but I was told I'd need to buy a pair of brown ExtraTough rain boots, which I had already noticed were highly fashionable here. Right when I stepped through the heavy plastic strip curtain, the Japanese man in charge welcomed me with a grunt and a finger telling me to, "Pick." As I followed the direction of his finger, the truth of all of the stories I had been told materialized. There I was, standing on a rubber mat, around a large bin of salmon eggs reaching for a pair of surgical tweezers. The three other women at my station happily chattered as they demonstrated how to pick mostly worms, but also any foreign matter out of the salmon eggs. They whispered about the final value of the product as if it was some sort of Japanese cabal whose sinister plot was to have minimum wage workers pick tapeworms out of their expensive caviar. They pointed out the small white pints with cute salmon labels, which retailed for a thousand dollars each in Japan. The two grumpy supervisors stood there in white aprons with their arms crossed as they watched over their production line and their pints that passed one by one on the conveyor belt out an opening in the wall. We swished our tweezers around in the water while cleaning, picking, repeating, and talking about nothing in particular all day long.

When we finished one batch of eggs, the men would come carry off the bin and replace it with a bucketful of new eggs. I looked around, realizing I would need to get to the rubbing tables in order to diversify my eighteen hour day. This is where the salmon egg sacks were punctured by hand while rubbing them back and forth along chicken wire. The eggs would fall through, and the slimy sack would stay on top like some sort of real-life Playdough. I had seen how it was done. Use cotton gloves and rub. There was only one woman working at the rubbing tables whom I was told was Lexi. In order to be like her they said I'd have to demonstrate good and submissive behavior. Not exactly my style, but I was committed to doing my best.

During break, I tumbled outside towards my girls who were now coming over to visit on my breaks and lunch whenever possible. Feeling giddy, I was singing the Beatles song, "I am the egg man, I am the egg man, I am the walrus, koo koo ka choo[4]," unable to get it out of my head. The girls still didn't have solid work and asked me how it was, "in there." I shared my new goal, to work the mucous membranes.

On the morning of day three, I took matters into my own hands, and I deadheaded to the rubbing tables. Everything was going well. I had my Walkman on and was getting into a groove at my self-appointed new station. I was stretching and moving as I sent my eggs through, playing a bit with my growing ball of mucous membranes. My fingertips were getting slightly numb from the cold and the chicken wire, but I held my ground a solid few days. It was when I got tired of waiting for someone to bring me more egg sacks and initiated lifting the bucket across the room myself that the Japanese blew the whistle on me, an actual whistle, and pointed to the other side of the room, sending me back to the picking tables.

It was unclear if they were against women lifting or didn't think women could possibly decipher between the various classes of eggs

---

[4] The Beatles, "I Am The Walrus", B-side to single *Hello, Goodbye*, Odeon, 1967, vinyl

(even though it was written on the side of the bucket in big black letters Gold A, A, B), or maybe it was our feminine energy in general that should not be handling the eggs. But Lexi, who I was quickly becoming friends with, was allowed to carry the buckets. This of course, gave everyone something new to talk about at the picking tables.

Lexi was an athletic young woman who worked as a ski instructor in Colorado during the winter and with the Alaskan Egg Men in the summer. I was trying to arrange moving into her dorm room through Jerry, the man who had hired me and was also in charge of the large home that had been converted into our cannery's bunkhouse. It seemed everything was in place to move over as soon as I found the time after my long workday. The cost would be $200 a month or **$6.66** per day, a sign that I knowingly disregarded. When I finally did make the time to break my tent down and move myself over, another woman had shifted rooms and took the good room with the cool girls that I really liked. Her move had created space in a room with two older Filipino women, and I quickly discovered why she had leapt at the opportunity to move out.

I was open and friendly towards my new roommates, but they barely spoke English. The younger of the two was named Jasmine, and she seemed friendly enough. The older woman was named Rowena. She had a grumpy, wrinkled face, and she set about huffing and puffing as to where I should put my things. She made a few things clear by pointing and saying, "You, No!" I was not to touch any of their things, especially their food items that were set up over

Rowena's upper bunk giving the room the look and smell of a small Asian grocery store. I set my backpack on the top bunk over Jasmine's bed who was still smiling which I took to mean, "Don't pay her any attention. That's just the way she is." With my gentler line of questioning, I was able to gather that they worked in the shrimp department together. Needing to get back to the egg room, I hardly had time to wonder how this was going to work out. Plus, working eighteen hour days, I was only getting four or five hours of sleep per night, so my brain was no longer functioning properly.

I was about a month in, and the same cycle continued. A few days at the rubbing tables, then I'd take some initiative to see where I stood with my lifting status, which was met with the twweeettttt of the whistle. Then it was back to the picking tables for me. This particular time, it seemed more serious though. The taller, angrier man was shouting at me in Japanese and the shorter, stockier one who spoke more English came to translate what seemed to be a final message.

"You NO lift! You NO rub! you PICK!"

I pointed to Lexi, who was lifting in that exact moment. "She Lexi, you NO, you PICK!"

It seemed they had completely lost their patience with me, and I was being banished from the rubbing tables to the tweezer table to pick at tapeworms *forever*. With all of my mucous membrane hopes dashed, the injustice of not being allowed to work just as hard as the men or take any sort of initiative boiled up to the surface. This was fucking ridiculous! Without thinking about it being one of the only available jobs on the island, I shouted, "I quit!" With my arms flailing, I stormed off. Now *that* would give them something to talk about at the picking tables for the rest of the day. I walked outside and began shaking, a combination of exhaustion and a Japanese induced angry adrenaline rush.

Chapter 5

Superpowers?

After I stomped out of the Egg Room, I went to the office to talk to Jerry. I marched there still fuming, thinking that if I explained that *sexism* was my reason for quitting, maybe the Japanese would be reprimanded, something would change, or in the very least I'd be compensated in some way. Jerry acknowledged and sympathized with my allegations of sexism but explained that there was nothing he or the cannery could do. The Japanese leased that department separately and legally they had nothing to do with the cannery itself. He further explained that if I wasn't able to find another job with the same company, and that, "No, there was nothing currently available," I'd have to move out of the bunkhouse, which would mean back to Tent City for me.

I went and sat on a bench that overlooked the boat harbor, still ruminating and meditating on my next possible move. Feeling the slow pace of this small fishing town, the song, "Sittin' on the dock of the bay, wastin' time"[5] was playing in my head, when Trent (one of Big B's close friends), a prematurely balding twenty-five-year-old who was very cute with a hat on, meandered by. Trent introduced me to his friend and boss, Max whom I had never met before. They worked in the freezer department together. When they asked what I was up to, I jumped right into all the Japanese details, being sure to emphasize the irony of being punished for taking initiative at work. Max said he could offer me a job if I was interested in working nights. I would work less, a guaranteed twelve hour schedule, but get paid more hourly as a nocturnal worker. He warned it was hard work. I would be the only girl, and I would have to pull my weight. Throughout the egg department suppression, I was beginning to discover that the two little words, *you can't* were what was fueling my rebellion in a big way. These two words would nearly always conjure the same response of, "Oh no!? Just watch me then!" So, the prospect of working a blue-collar job with all men, and working just as hard as them, was now exactly what I was looking for. And it was with the same cannery, which meant keeping my housing too. Max told me to come see him sometime within the next few days if I was interested, which I assured him that, "Yes, yes, yes!" I was. He gave me his business card, and I filed it into my George Costanza sized wallet which I kept in my back pocket. I couldn't believe my good fortune! It seemed I had landed another job that very same day. Previously exhausted, the Universe now had my attention, waking me up once again. I felt as if my heart was lifting right out of my body in gratitude, yet I didn't know exactly

---

[5] Otis Redding, "The Dock Of The Bay", track #1 on *(Sittin' On) The Dock of the Bay*, Volt/Atco, 1968, vinyl

where I was sending it. In fact, the degree to which I seemed to be co-creating my reality was getting to be alarming because it seemed too good to be true. Something big was happening here, at least to me, and no one else seemed to be noticing.

Pleased with myself, I decided to call it a day and headed to the pizzeria for the first time in over a month since I'd started work in the egg department. I had a ton of news to share, but the big brothers were just focused on what a dipshit Max was. According to them, he just sat at the supervisor's desk upstairs with his girlfriend all night while Trent worked his ass off down in the freezers. Unphased, and realizing I probably wasn't going to find my dream job in Petersburg, Alaska anyway, I pulled out Max's business card to admire it. I set about organizing the state of my wallet while I waited for the girls to arrive and low and behold, in the depths of random contacts and receipts, I found the magical piece of paper that I was searching for in my Chico apartment … the liquid LSD! I hadn't thought to look in my wallet because I didn't realize it was on a business card. Wooooo Hoooooo! I could hardly contain myself.

Every time I took psychedelics, they seemed to provide me with more answers. It was so interesting that they were showing up again on this particular day just when I had more questions arising around *how* or *why* a string of fortunate events continued happening to me. The exact same day I landed a second job in a town where supposedly there was no work, I also found my misplaced LSD (something else that was unheard of this area at that time). It now seemed this substance was waiting until this precise moment to present itself to me. If I had known where it was over a month ago, it would have been long gone. I was so excited. I wiggled back and forth in my bar stool doing a victory dance as I began showing the guys the visible wet stain on the card that looked to contain about five or six hits. Big B wasn't interested in partaking, but Russel and their other good friend Graham were. Big B offered to drive us up to the top of a mountain peak where there were 360 degree views atop a garnet mine. Once the girls arrived, we ate pizza and formulated a plan to rescue Trent from the freezers and set off for the mountain top.

Upon arrival, my attention moved in phases from the view to the round garnets in the dirt, back to the view again. We were all gathering these naturally faceted semi-precious gemstones as we periodically took in the orange ocean sunset. Gradually, our attention moved from the garnets to stuffing our faces with wild blueberries and then to a steep trail, mossy trees and a creek down below. I used what I told Jana were my magical powers to run down the steep trail laughing while she was screaming at the top for help to get down. At one point, Russell began to walk along a wide fallen tree trunk like a monkey scratching under his arms and howling at the rest of us. We all wandered in our own worlds of love and laughter until we naturally began descending from the high and then off the mountain top as well. On our drive down the dirt road, we had porcupines waddling ahead of us in the headlights, their quills flying out in self-defense. Big B stopped the car to show us the quills, knowing that all of us girls were crafty "bead-a-holics" as we called ourselves. He explained how Alaskan Natives use the hollow quills in their traditional beadwork.

We gathered yet another natural commodity before we continued the rest of the way "home" with garnet filled pockets, ending what had turned out to be one of the most playful, magical nights of my life. It hadn't brought any particular clarity, but was pure, high-spirited unadulterated joy. Having been up all night and then sleeping all day was a perfect transition to working the night shift.

The night freeze wasn't rocket science. Trent took me under his wing teaching me how to use a pallet jack and move the thousand pound (plus) fish totes around by hand. We'd stack whole salmon on tall racks with trays, wheel them into the freezer and write the time on the chalkboard to know when they'd be done. We broke down the freezer on the other side, mostly working with the day shift's fish, sending them through a glaze tank, packing and weighing them in fifty pound boxes. This was all done to very loud punk rock or heavy metal music. Dipshit would not be my choice of words, but Max was clearly not present at all. Early on, when the Metallica CD was skipping, they sent me upstairs to tell him to change the music and sure enough, there he was, feet up on the desk, watching a movie and making out with his girlfriend.

Trent was basically in charge, and once I understood how to read the chalkboards, my new coworkers also looked to me for direction. After I had gained confidence and the work was becoming brainless, I decided I could go to work stoned. It would actually help to pass the time. One day after a smoke break, Trent put me at the scale, and the fish started coming. I had half a pound leeway which meant the boxes had to weigh between 49.5 and 50.5

pounds, but all the fish weighed in at around nine pounds, making it impossible to reach this weight. Their weight only varied by the tiniest fraction of a pound. I had never experienced anything like this so far.

The frozen fish began to pile up on the conveyor belt, until they had to flip the emergency switch on the glaze tank to stop feeding the salmon through. I spun around in blazed circles trying to eyeball six smaller fish or four larger, unsure if I had already tried those same fish before. No matter what, I was still two pounds off. It was impossible. By then, a few of the Latin crew members started sliding fish boxes around at my feet, trying to help and free up the conveyor belt to keep the glaze tank running. Max must have heard the buzzer sound on the emergency stop because he came downstairs to see what was going on. He took one look at my eyes and (also a pot smoker) shook his head saying, "You're fucking stoned."

"Yes, but that's not it. All the fish weigh the same," I whined. "You try it!" We wheeled out more racks from the freezer, but all these fish were close to that exact same size. We couldn't make it work. Max explained that fish that swam in the same school were usually the exact same size and weight, and that the entire batch must have been caught together. Until the next freezer batch was ready, there was nothing we could do. We were in a salmon stalemate and all free to go home early at 3:00 a.m. That meant more sleep and longer daytime hours to get things done.

With little work still, the girls were thinking about leaving. Eva was considering traveling to mainland Alaska to the bluegrass music festivals with a friend. Cami had just found out she was pregnant with a boy from back home, and Jana was homesick, even though she had landed herself an extremely good looking guy who also worked at my cannery. His good looks were accompanied with arrogance as he began bragging about his lifestyle between make-out sessions with Jana at evening break time. He worked in Alaska in the summer and spent his winters in Mexico, "Living like a king." The year prior, he had made a new discovery. Costa Rica. "The best place on earth. Beautiful women, cheap beer, incredible rain forest, blah blah blah." I was completely turned off by his chauvinistic description, but the Big Bros were all ears. He lived in and drove his VW camper van down south, but these mid-twenty-year-olds wanted to know how much a plane ticket would be and what the actual cost of living was. Uninterested, as he went on to describe the cost of beer and a plate of food, I began to think back to our day trips to Tijuana where my parents had taken us every year when we were kids. It was cheap, and I loved experiencing another culture, the art, the language, the food and music. I had wanted to travel but revisiting Latin America on my own as an adult was something I had never really considered. I was now being shown it was attainable, and I added this to my mental Rolodex of possibilities.

After work early one morning as I walked up the wooden steps to the bunkhouse, I noticed a terrible smell. There was a black garbage bag on the front porch that had flies swarming all around it. My roommates were just waking up as I tiptoed into our room, grabbed my towel and headed to the shower. As I undressed, I flexed my biceps in the mirror, admiring the "man arms" I was getting from the little time I had spent on the night crew. Arms well suited for my men's work shirt, which was a light blue button up that looked like it had belonged to a mechanic with the name *Mack* on the patch across my chest. After showering, I made my way back into the bedroom wrapped in my towel, planning to dress in my cutest most comfortable pair of overalls. They had purple and silver moon designs on the pockets and the trim but were nowhere to be found. In fact, none of my clothes were in the closet. I marched out into the kitchen in my towel where Jasmine and Rowena were cooking their breakfast. I had tried really hard to be friendly to them, but no matter what I did, they didn't seem to like me. "What did you do with my clothes?" I demanded to know.

"Dirty? Dirty clothes?" the eldest responded, always the ring leader. Jasmine just seemed to get bullied into going along with Rowena's shriveled up old attitude.

"They were not dirty," I shouted. "I need clean clothes to put on and now I have no clothes!"

"Dirty. Smell." Rowena scrunched up her face and plugged her nose as she pointed to the front door and said, "Outside."

I ran out to the stinky black garbage bag covered in flies, which contained all my clothes, dirty mixed with clean, and rummaged around for my overalls. Now all my clean clothes had touched my dirty fish factory clothes that I had quarantined in the garbage bag tied up in our closet. Damn it! I'd have to wash them all. I stormed past the kitchen as Rowena made further attempts to poke and jab, telling me I needed to go to the laundromat. "OKaayyyy," I barked back. "But it's not open until nine. You think you smell like *flowers* working with shrimp all day!? How do *your* clothes *not* smell?"

"Wash clothes at laundromat," she repeated, and I wasn't sure if they washed their clothes at the laundromat *every day* or she was continuing to tell me what I needed to do.

I just wanted them to go to work so I could prepare dinner in the kitchen and fall asleep in my underwear, which was now the only cleanish thing I owned. I'd have to wake up by 2:00 p.m. to have enough time to wash clothes and be back at work by six.

Trent's girlfriend put her car on the island ferry, leaving on the same boat that my girlfriends did, and he and I began to work more closely together. We were back to smoking weed on break now that we had the big fish/small fish dilemma dialed in and knew to be sure to stack a variety of different sized salmon for each freeze. We would go to the Greasy Spoon restaurant together some mornings after work, ordering breakfast for our dinner. Trent would have a few beers, which seemed odd at 6:30 a.m. I was lamenting about my roommates over dinner one morning, dramatically explaining the laundry issue. Laughing, Trent told me that I had to admit it was pretty funny, especially since I had said how bad the smell was on the front porch. But he clearly didn't understand the whole dynamic. He and I were becoming good friends, sharing an experience together that summer, laughing, and feeling a mutual attraction. Before too long, we also shared our first kiss, and knowing full well about my bunking situation, he came home with me just to sleep and snuggle once they went off to work for the day.

We both fell asleep exhausted, fully clothed in my little bunk bed. I should have put Trent on the inside, against the wall because when my roommates came home for lunch, we woke up to Jasmine screaming, "MAN! MAN! Man in my bed!" She was yelling as if he was actually in *her* bed, not asleep on the top bunk with me. Now it was my turn to laugh as Trent went running through the bunkhouse with Rowena close behind, her hands up over her head, shouting in Filipino. Shortly after, I was having another conversation with Jerry, this time being reprimanded and told I would have to leave the bunkhouse if there was ever a man in our room again. "It's not fair," I complained. "They completely over-react to *everything*! Do you know that they threw all my clothes outside in a garbage bag?"

When Jerry put two and two together, he started laughing. "Those were your **clothes**? I remember that bag. It *did* smell really bad." It was clear I was getting nowhere, and he reminded me that I was staying in a *girls'* bunk room. No men, or I'd be out.

Tired of my living situation, and with my weed supply getting dangerously low, I set out to do a bit of research. I called my best friend Jocelyn in Southern California, describing the scarcity and the price of weed in Petersburg. I asked her if she could send me more General Delivery to the post office. If I was able to sell weed on the island, I might quit my cannery job and stay a bit longer. She was too nervous, explaining that the Oklahoma City bombing and news of heightened security was all everyone was talking about, something I was completely unaware of. Without more weed, I didn't know how much longer I wanted to stay.

Not knowing what my next move would be, I called home to check in with my family and received surprising news all around. First, my mother told me that Jerry Garcia had died. This came as a terrible blow as I knew it would put an end to an entire subculture and my chances of ever joining in their magical caravan full-time. My mom also told me that my father was being transferred from our Southern Californian home to Miami for work, where he would be in charge of (and therefore travel more) their Latin American accounts. This was a very interesting yet unexpected turn of events. Contrary to my sister being devastated by this news because it meant she would be transferring high schools, it made me think that an uprooting like this must be exactly what I needed. Their moving would shake things up and force me to spread my wings in new directions away from my usual stomping grounds on the West Coast and in California.

My mother also said with the stress of the move, my sister's horrible reaction to it, and my being in Alaska, she had broken down and called a psychic woman that my aunt had recommended. Now *this* was out of character. She recounted a bit of their conversation but said that the single most interesting thing the woman had told her was to not worry about her oldest daughter. The psychic sensed that I was far away from her, but she went on to explain that anything I got myself into, I would always come out smelling like roses. "Amen," I said jokingly, and we shared a laugh before we said our goodbyes.

My mom was shocked by this woman's accuracy with my having gone to work in a fish factory, and okay, yes, my clothes smelled bad, but everything *had* worked out for me so well that I *did* come out smelling like roses. This was more confirmation that the stars were somehow aligning for me and even reaching out and penetrating my family, but all of these synchronicities coming together at once became overwhelming. I began to feel as if my life was moving in slow motion, like I was in some kind of surreal movie wherein I was my own director choosing the setting, plot and characters. Even Rowenda and Jasmine had added some necessary conflict to my storyline, or perhaps I was playing out *my* role in *their* independent films. Now, I began to wonder if I wasn't tapping into some kind of psychic abilities myself. *Was I developing magical powers, or have guardian angels helping to orchestrate the highest good in my life? Or maybe I was just too high all together? Was I some kind of white witch or maybe a fairy? I love fairies!* There were so many unknowns that I began to wonder if what I had started to tap into had to do with the "occult"; crystal balls, tarot cards or Ouija boards in any way. I knew that I was still operating out of love, but societal doubt and pressure now came bubbling up. *Is this why Christianity and authorities warn against these things? Are they somehow connected to darkness? Maybe there is a lot of supernatural power available to all of us (good and bad), or maybe I'm actually losing my mind.*

I didn't know it at the time, but the word psychedelic was formed by combining the Greek words psyche (mind, soul, self) and dēlos (to clear, to manifest), so mind or soul clearing/manifesting which does perfectly describe the experiences I was having. Not only had I been using a lot of psycho-active substances at this time, I had also completely eliminated (or cleared) exterior distractions in my life which brought about greater awareness, allowing me to actually witness my mind and what I was manifesting. Television and technology were non-existent in my world, and it's not as if I had a busy schedule rushing from appointment to appointment with my mind spinning. I had no social life. In fact, I was spending most of my time alone. In addition to eliminating stress and distractions from my life, I was also intentional about what I was consuming. I listened to and often sang highly positive uplifting music. I was living at a very slow pace, walking everywhere I went; eating wild berries, and absorbing the beautiful nature all around me. The sky and tree tops were full of bald eagles, I'd see an occasional bear, spectacular mountain and ocean views, and the picturesque boat harbor. I was aligning my energy to all of this, mindful and receptive to what the present moment might have in store.

I also didn't realize that psychoactive substances have been known to induce paranormal experiences meaning extra sensory perception (ESP), telepathy, precognition, clairvoyance, etc. In fact, a woman named Linnda Caporael hypothesized that ergot (what LSD is derived from) poisoning may have caused the "witchy" behavior of some of the women killed in the Salem Witch Trials.[6] So thinking I was a witch or developing some sort of magical powers maybe wasn't that far off, but at that time, I really

---

[6] Linnda R. Caporael "Ergotism: The Satan Loosed in Salem?" Science Vol. 192, April 1976

had no one I could share any of this with. My friends had left the island, but besides, even when they were there, it somehow seemed more egotistical than crazy to verbalize that I thought I was a witch or a fairy. And although they had also dabbled with these substances, they seemed like they were able to turn off again and all go back to life as usual. Feeling like I had no one to talk to, I just blurted all of this out to a complete stranger while sitting on my favorite bench overlooking the boat harbor one day.

We went from, "I'm from California," to "Have you ever felt as if you are creating your own reality?" After a brief description of how my planlessness had led to greater opportunities that summer, all of my questions came tumbling out at once. "Maybe I'm developing some sort of sixth sense? Maybe I'm opening to subtle energies that cannot be seen? If I'm a white witch playing with light energy, could I also somehow be opening myself up to darkness and evil? Is that the reason more people aren't willing to explore reality? Fear of the unknown? Of darkness?" This man was very sweet and gently chuckled, first holding out his hand to shake mine, "Hello, I'm Mark by the way." Then, he admitted that no, truthfully he had never experienced what I was describing, but he offered something else. He said that I reminded him of another woman he had once met. She was also free-spirited and refused to settle for a "normal life" and instead was traveling indefinitely. She called herself a *flutterby*, someone who moves from place to place spreading joy for a short while and then moving on. This was definitely relatable, and even though Mark didn't provide answers about the supernatural phenomena I was experiencing, I felt heard, and this was enough to move forward with a little more self-acceptance and less fear that I was going crazy.

Feeling ready to flutter on myself, I decided to go to the ferry office to see when the next boat would be leaving the island. There was a boat scheduled to leave in twelve days' time and then there wouldn't be another for over a month. I didn't think I could take much more of fish freezing, and besides, the ground would be starting to freeze here soon as well. I purchased a ticket to Bellingham, Washington on the next boat and then worked up until the last night before my departure. I said my goodbyes to Trent and cannery friends and walked down to the boat docks to board the ferry. Just as I was finishing pitching my tent on the upper boat deck, I looked up to see Chico Shane boarding the ship. Waving, I caught his attention, and he made his way up the stairs to my temporary campsite. With this being the last ship to set sail before *his* fall term in Chico started, I had assumed he'd be on this ferry, but without a way to communicate with him, I was trusting that if it was meant to be, it would be. And here he was. The perfect way to end such a serendipitous summer. We hugged, and as the ferry pulled away, the sun came out in full force, burning off the drizzly rain and fog for the first time all summer. We sat on the white plastic seats with our feet up on the rail. "Well," he asked, "How was your summer?"

Laughing, I responded with, "Working in the fish canneries was an *experience*, not necessarily a *good* experience, but an experience." I went on to say that I'd probably never do it again. I definitely saw more in my future than factory work. Especially fish factory work, but it was certainly an adventure. "I'd love to come back and see more of Alaska. Maybe I'll return to sell weed next summer, and then travel to Costa Rica for the winter." Over the next two days, the boat moved slowly through the Inside Passage, a protected marine highway that flows between Southeast Alaska and a multitude of islands, which sadly, were mostly logged. Shane and I shared the journey (and my tent platonically) together, and I felt that rather than fluttering, I was being gently pulled, as if magnetically, towards my next adventure.

Chapter 6

Darker Days

S hane and I made friends with a few young guys on the ferry who told us about the up and coming Seattle Hemp Festival. They invited us to stay at their house in the mountains northeast of Seattle until the festival started the following weekend. Shane had to return to school and went directly to the Greyhound bus station, but I took them up on their offer. I remember camping in their backyard, but the days leading up to Hempfest were pretty much a blur of bong tokes and cooking vegetarian meals together. Hempfest 1995 was held at the oceanfront Myrtle Edwards Park and exceeded any lack of expectations I had, which was something else I was coming to realize. Releasing any expectations about future outcomes, especially the "how" things would happen would usually result in some kind of greater magic or opportunity that I could have never dreamed up on my own, such as an invitation to Seattle HempFest, which prior to the ferry ride, I had never known existed.

I had embraced Peter Tosh's lyrics to "Legalize It" and what I had understood to be cannabis culture at that time, but this was my first introduction to the movement and to the people on the front line who were actually working to legalize marijuana. At HempFest there were educational booths, petitions to sign, and everyone was handing out non psychoactive cannabis joints. I knew of the many uses and benefits of hemp and marijuana, and I also knew that the government's rejection of this medicinal plant was ill-founded. But what I hadn't realized was the depth of their intentionality regarding these policies. Jack Herer, the leading cannabis rights activist and the author of *The Emperor Wears No Clothes* was there and openly chatting about the petrochemical industry's plot to outlaw this renewable resource for paper, energy, food, textiles, and medicine. Otherwise, friendly hippie ladies were there shouting about the U.S. government *knowingly* misinforming the public about marijuana. "There have been countless studies done proving that marijuana is *not* a dangerous substance, *nor* a gateway drug, which lawmakers chose to ignore!" And then there was the fact that marijuana prohibition was and still is a racist policy which purposefully targeted Blacks, Mexicans, and later, hippies. This was the first time I had met actual changemakers; people who were on the ground, fighting to legalize marijuana. Aside from knowing it *should* be legalized, and a plethora of other social and ecological injustices that *should* be changed, I had never really given much thought as to how or who was ever going to make these things happen. I was truly inspired, and also added this to a growing list of possibilities for myself. After listening to a variety of guest speakers and mostly punk bands, the sun began to set. My choices as I saw them were to either sleep on the streets of Seattle or make my way back to California where I had friends and a support network of couches I could sleep upon. I decided to make my way to the Greyhound bus station and bought a direct ticket to Chico, California.

When the bus pulled into the Portland station in the middle of the night, I went outside to smoke a cigarette. There was over an hour wait before I could transfer to another bus. I was sitting outside on the pavement with my back to the station wall when a middle aged African American man dressed in baggy pants and a worn-out U.S. Military camouflage jacket engaged me in conversation. He first inquired about my travels, and when I mentioned Alaska, he coaxed me along asking what I was doing there. I told him I was working in the fish canneries, and he lit up saying, "You can make a lot of money doing that! How much did you make?" Out of pride for how much I had actually managed to save, I openly told him I had made $2,000. "Are you carrying that much money?" He wanted to know, which was a definite red flag, but, no I wasn't, so what was the harm in telling him no?

"Well, maybe you can help me out though," he went on to say. He told me he was carrying a lot of money which made him nervous, and there was something he needed to go run and do. He proceeded to pull out a large sum of money folded over, and rubber banded together from inside his coat pocket. There was a twenty-dollar bill visible on the outside. He asked how much money I was carrying, which I responded to, telling him $300. He wanted me to hold on to his money while he was gone, but asked to see my money just to be sure I actually had money of my own and wouldn't be tempted to steal his. And yes, I wanted to do the nonracist thing here and trust this man, so I opened up my wallet and showed him my money. From here, he suggested we put our money together so I was also invested and would be sure to protect his riches while he was away. This was somehow very convincing, so I handed over all the money I was carrying and watched him rubber band my money to the outside of his huge bundle. He demonstrated how to place it inside my jacket to "keep it real safe," tucking it momentarily inside his pocket before handing his savings along with his faith over to me. He left saying he would return shortly, and I sat and bathed in the honor I felt that this man would trust me with such a large amount of money for about five seconds. That thought was immediately followed by how strange it was of a total stranger to supposedly hand over a thousand dollars to me.

I quickly checked the stack of bills he had left me, ripping off the rubber band. There was a twenty-dollar bill on the outside, but the inside was just magazine clippings in perfectly cut rectangles. Angry and embarrassed, I sprang to my feet leaving my backpack on the ground against the wall. I looked around the corner and down the dark street in what seemed to be a pretty sketchy area of the city, but he was nowhere in sight. There would be little use in running around this neighborhood looking for this man with my backpack on. In fact, it could result in worse. I thought to cut my loses and go inside to talk to a security guard.

I could see the two middle aged, overweight security guards through the large glass windows of the office, but the doors were locked (probably for their own security). So, I proceeded to knock and wait. They let me in, listened to, and then laughed at my story. "The old Jamaican switch, and you fell for it!" Shaking their heads in disbelief, they asked why I would trust that man with my money and what I wanted them to do about it. "Are you prepared to wait around to file a police report and possibly miss your bus? You will never see that man or your money again."

This was less than helpful. It was hurtful, as I already felt bad enough about my own gullibility. My suggestion that, "Maybe you are familiar with this gentleman? Know his name?" was only met with more cynicism, as apparently these incidences go on day and night here. "You're lucky it wasn't worse, that he didn't have a gun or a knife. He just tricked you, that's all," he toned down his chuckling as he saw my distress shifting from sadness to anger that was directed at him. It was obvious they couldn't be bothered, and I left feeling completely embarrassed and frustrated, plopping down to continue waiting for my bus safely on the hard plastic chairs. I was nearly in tears. Now after all my hard work in Alaska, I had two thousand dollars, minus three hundred in a snap.

My next financial blow came in Chico. It began as a way to make back the money that had been stolen, by buying an ounce of weed for resale purposes. I was staying with Holding, and he organized the deal. It was with a young white woman named Sharon who was presumably a college student because she was our age, but I had never met her before. She came to the house and showed me the weed in a large Ziplock bag. I didn't get a very good vibe from her and thought she probably had feelings for Holding as well, or the bag was possibly short. He and I checked the weight on a scale in his room, and it was fine. I pinched off a small bud and grabbed my money as Holding tucked the ounce away in his backpack as a temporary hiding place. We returned to smoke a bowl with her and chatted about the upcoming Halloween party our group of friends was all going to, asking if she would be there as well. He and I talked about our costumes and maybe taking mushrooms there together, but she seemed distant, sketchy even, and left right away.

I had sold $60 worth of weed and smoked at least that much with friends, leading up to and during the pre-Halloween party Holding had hosted at his bachelor pad. Until this point, I had been sleeping on these guys' couch, slowly working my way back into Holding's life. I had sent him a few postcards while I was away, and now we were sharing our stories from summer with one another and spending most of his free time together (I was always free). There was still a closeness and a mutual attraction between us, but when I addressed it, he was slow and guarded with me. He said he didn't want to ruin our friendship. The night of the Halloween party he was drunk, and I initiated finally sleeping together in his room. I was sober and hopeful, but he had drank too much and it was quick, leaving me disappointed and wanting a longer, deeper connection all around. The next morning, I made an attempt to have a conversation about it. Lying in his bed, I watched him getting dressed and sleepily confessed, "I'm glad that happened, but it was really quick."

"You should have been drunk, too," was his unexpected, shallow response.

"Or," I replied, "We could both be sober next time and start making it a more regular thing."

"I have to go to work," he said, cutting me off as he finished buttoning up his jeans and headed out the door to his landscaping job.

I was still glad it did finally happen, and feeling puzzled by his distance, I got out of bed aiming to wake and bake. That would surely bring about more perspective. I made my may to Holding's backpack where we had hidden my weed and was horrified to find all of my stash gone. All $350 worth, minus the little I had sold and smoked. This gave my mind a lot more than last night's events to work with. Thinking he may have moved our hiding place, I waited for Holding to come home, trying my best not to put too much energy into the worst case scenario. But no, he was more shocked than I was at that point, having just heard the news. Pacing the living room, he deduced that the only person, aside from his roommates who we trusted, that had seen where he hid the weed was Sharon, the woman who had sold it to me. She also knew we were going to be away at the Halloween party. He called and called her landline, but she never answered. Then, it felt as if he was unreachable as well. Deflated from having a total of over $600 of my hard-earned fishing money stolen, and now getting absolutely no warm and fuzzy relationship feelings from Holding, I was back to sleeping on his couch once again.

Holding had had his heart broken by his high school girlfriend, Lily, who also lived in Chico and was in my same circle of girlfriends. Even though I really liked Lily, I couldn't help feeling jealous of her. She was drop dead gorgeous in this cute little blonde Disney cartoon kind of way and was still in his life, coming by the house quite often. She and I spent some time together, and I confessed my feelings to her about Holding, half seeking advice and half asking if they still had feelings for one another. She reassured me there was nothing going on between the two of them and encouraged me to be patient with him. But since I didn't actually have a place to live to *be* patient, I decided to move on. He knew how I felt about him, and that he was welcome to collaborate with me on my vision for the next great Alaskan adventure; to save enough money to buy a large quantity of marijuana and go back to Alaska the following summer.

I couch surfed on over to a girlfriends' huge bachelorette pad, and now I was feeling comfortable enough to try to engage everyone in discussions about the esoteric discoveries that I had been making such as life is a movie, we are creating our own reality, and nothing in the material world is actually real. More than one person told me that I sounded like our friend, Little Lisa who by talking about the same sort of things, had landed herself in a mental hospital. Now this got my attention! And I wanted to know exactly what she had been talking about, who had her committed and where she was now.

I pieced together that our cute little dreadlocked, nose pierced friend had been eating dirt and talking about returning to Mother Earth, so her parents came and took her to a mental hospital. After she got out, she had tried to set herself on fire in their family garage. I was shocked! I couldn't believe that our friends, *my* friends, or her boyfriend couldn't have just talked her down and brought her back without having to call her parents or having her committed. "He tried," Sue, one of the bachelorettes explained. "She had taken acid together with her boyfriend. That's what initiated her dirt eating. For three days he took care of her and tried to talk her down, but she never fully came back. He had to get back to his life and school, so he called her parents." This was the only person or events that I had heard about that sounded remotely like anything I had been experiencing. I wanted to learn more about what had happened. I also wanted to see how she was doing and if there was any way I could help, so I tracked down her parents' phone number.

Her mother answered the phone and said Lisa still wasn't in any condition to talk to friends. I explained that I had just heard this news and had been living and working in Alaska all summer. I said I wasn't in school and that I wanted to come there and visit her daughter. "I think it would be good for her," I added. "I have had some of the same thoughts and experiences that I heard Lisa has been having. I've felt a closeness to the Earth or a higher power that made it hard for me to relate to *normal* life. I think I could talk to her. I think it might help." Her mother agreed and gave me directions to their home in Walnut Creek.

After a long "layover" in Sacramento, a number of buses, and walking the rest of the way, I arrived to find Lisa shell shocked, wearing a pair of thick compression socks to treat the burns on her legs. She didn't know what she was doing when she started the fire, she said openly with her mother in earshot. She wanted to burn away all the thoughts she was having. She thought maybe she could cleanse her soul through fire. She said all she could see was the flames, still. That she was still in that place of darkness, with flames all around her, wanting to end her confusion.

"Okay, that's enough Lisa," her mother intervened. "You nearly killed yourself, *and* burned the house down, and you *know* how you did it, with gasoline and a match. But you are *not* still in that fire. And please please please don't ever do that or anything like it again." But I understood what Lisa had meant, and we locked eyes. I hadn't realized just what I would be stepping into, and it was hard to know what to say with her mom hovering there. She had obviously adopted a different rehabilitation program than I had thought to implement. I wanted to hear exactly what Lisa was experiencing to see how I could relate and help her feel understood. Her mother seemed to be pushing Lisa's experiences away, ignoring her craziness so she could move forward and get better. "No, I understand," I said staring into her beautiful little face. But other than that, it was difficult to have a conversation with Lisa. Aside from still being in that fire, she was highly medicated, and her mother kept her busy journaling, watching special videos, and going to therapy. I hadn't known Lisa that well before this, and now it was impossible to get to know her better with her mother supervising our visitation.

I spent most of my time there alone, journaling or sketching at their kitchen table, quickly becoming bored. Lisa commented that she liked my drawings, but by the end of the second full day, I wondered what I was really doing there. I told her I would probably be leaving the next morning, which was met with a blank stare. I added that I wanted to visit her because I had had some of the same realizations she did and that for a while I thought I was going crazy, too or that maybe I was a witch or something. A tiny light went on. "So, what can we do… what can *I* do?" she asked. "I don't know," I shrugged. "Ride it out? Act normal? I'm personally curious to see where it leads me, but *don't* set fire to yourself or anything else. There is nothing wrong with you. You're beautiful on the inside and the outside, and things *will* get better." Both she and her mother seemed okay with this, but nothing more was said.

When I went to leave the next morning, after some prompting from her mom, Lisa thanked me for coming with an expressionless face. The whole thing was strange, and I wasn't really sure if I had helped at all. But as I saw it, I was also there gathering information about the psyche and myself. And even though I didn't know where I was headed in life, I now knew that a zombie-like existence was not my fate. In fact, I left unsure if Lisa and I *were* having the same experience. Though I had never really been exposed to psychosis or schizophrenia firsthand, and at that time I had no idea that those could be counterindications for using psychedelic substances, I did get the feeling that her mental health combined with psychedelics is what took her beyond an eight hour experience. Seeing Lisa in this state was in no way a warning to me against using these substances. To the contrary, it solidified my belief that I would always personally come back from every trip.

I returned to Chico, but all of my college friends, including Holding were thoroughly immersed in jobs and studies, and they had very little time to play. My bike had been stolen right before I went to Alaska, which now left me less mobile and free. With nearly half my summer earnings spent or stolen, I decided to continue on to visit friends in Southern California. I stayed there with high school friends until winter, spending all of my money, and then flew to Miami, Florida to visit my family in their new home for the holidays.

Chapter 7

Jah Provides

To my father's dismay, I flew across the country with the last of my fish money, just ten cents in my wallet. This completely went against his hard-working, importance-of-saving values that he had tried to instill within me. "Michelle, you cannot, nor should you travel across the country with just ten cents to your name. What if something were to happen? If you needed to buy food? Or medicine?" But *contraire mon frère*, I actually just *did,* and everything was fine!

I had one contact in Miami named Rodrigo or "Rod," a quirky, young, dreadlocked Puerto Rican who I had met in Tent City. Rod had made an impression on me when he had dropped to his knees in the middle of the walking path thanking Jah Rastafari for a late summer display of the northern lights. His extreme act of gratitude echoed how I felt not only in Alaska's nature but for every day, and I was happy to have at least one friend in Miami. We spoke on the phone, making plans to go to Key West for New Year's Eve, but when I shared this with my parents, my dad forbade me to go there in my sister's car. In his opinion, it was unnecessary to drive six hours round trip when there was plenty to do downtown Miami. He added that he would be checking the mileage and gave me a curfew of 3:00 a.m., "*at the latest.*" I relayed this to Rod, and he disagreed. Having grown up in Miami, I trusted him that Key West was absolutely where the party was. He had also planned to import weed there and had no car of his own, so our plans continued to move in that direction.

On New Year's Eve Rod showed up to my parents' house with his two friends Adrian and Juan. Adrian was the most inconspicuous of the three, dressed in well fitted jeans with a brand-new white t-shirt. Juan was a heavyset Haitian Cuban dressed in baggy jeans, an oversized t-shirt and a dark blue beanie pulled down low on his head. Later I would learn this was to cover a large scar on his forehead. As he leaned over my parents' kitchen counter, resting his large forearms with his hands clasped, I couldn't help noticing all his gold rings and the letters L-O-V-E tattooed across his knuckles. I mentioned the *LOVE* as my mother skeptically questioned Juan as to what he does for work. We were all pleasantly surprised when he offered the fact that he had been living in New York City working with a non-profit group his friend had started, helping her to convert her van into a food cart to feed the homeless. With my family's judgement shifting away from Juan's outward appearance towards his virtuous line of work, I saw our window to go, and we made our way to the front door. As my father walked us out, he informed me that he had checked the mileage and expected me home by 2:00 a.m. or 3:00 at the latest, "from a party in *Miami.*" As we headed South on the 1, the guys asked what my plan was. We were obviously going to Key West, so with visions of Ferris Bueller running the red convertible backwards on blocks I told them, "I'll cross that bridge later."

Our first stop was at Rod's dealers' house, which to my surprise, didn't live that far from my parents' upper middle-class neighborhood. They were a hippie couple in their late forties that lived in an older wooden home on a huge, overgrown jungle-like piece of property. With our first mission accomplished, I was driving once again while Rod loaded celebratory bowls in the passenger seat. The vibe was high as we all sang along to the top hits on the radio. "Here comes the hotstepper, Murderer, I'm the lyrical gangster, Murderer, Dial emergency number, Murderer, Still love you like that."[7] Mid-verse, my sister's white two door Hyundai Scoupe began to shake. Panicked, Juan reassured me that it was only a flat tire, and I was able to pull into a mini mart parking lot, now halfway to Key West. With three guys to help change the flat, it shouldn't of been a problem. The boys had all gone inside the store, leaving the car jacked up. They had taken the flat off but were yet to put the spare on. In an effort to prove myself a capable forward-thinking female, I took it upon myself to put the flat tire in the trunk. There was a little too much force and intention behind my action because as I shoved, trying to situate the tire against the back seat, the car began to move forward in slow motion, until eventually, it fell off the jack making a horrible metal crunching sound as it landed. All our hopes of it being "not that bad" were shattered as we pulled out of the

---

[7] Ini Kamoze, "Here Comes The Hotstepper", single, Columbia Records, 1994, CD

mini-mart with the tire finally changed, and the car started making a loud scraping sound. Juan surmised that the axel was bent, which was the perfect metaphor for what was about to happen to my relationship with my family; bend, if not break.

I didn't actually care about the car. It was merely a material possession, and all my parents' rules and restrictions were just limiting belief structures at this point. They lived in a world full of low vibrating, "you can't just (fill in the blank)" in what for me was a sea of highly charged possibilities. I did however, care about inconveniencing my sister by wrecking her car, and I certainly wasn't looking forward to the impending conversation around all of this that lay ahead with my parents, specifically my father. Juan asked if we should go back, knowing it would not be good for the car to continue. We discussed it, but we were more than halfway there now, so I made the final decision to keep moving forward and prolong my dad's inevitable infuriation. Juan drove the rest of the way, but it was impossible for me to put what had just happened out of my mind with the car screeching the entire time.

Once we parked the car and Rod gave me a surprise hit of acid, I was finally able to shift my attention away from future family meltdown scenarios to the present party moment we had been chasing. We walked to Duvall Street which was closed to traffic and where the legendary party Rod had promised was forming. Over thirty hippies were starting to gather, and their drum circle was gaining momentum. Rod and Adrian moved in and out amongst the crowd selling weed, and I began dancing around and within the circle. After hours of continuously dancing, I began to see and feel energy. I could feel electric raindrops tingling on the entire surface of my body. I could see this energy sparkling like white glittery rain in the atmosphere all around us. Juan watched with arms crossed from the sidelines like my personal bodyguard, quietly handing me a bottle of water at one point.

I danced all night long, and the guys' business venture proved to be successful. Just like Petersburg, Alaska because of its isolation, marijuana was harder to come by and more expensive in Key West. Throughout their transactions, the guys had learned that everyone in this drum circle hippie scene was going up to the Ocala Rainbow Gathering after New Year's and then to the Mississippi Gathering following that.

I was part of a new travel plan that the guys filled me in on during our sonorous drive back. Rod wanted to return to Key West with more product to sell so he offered to pay Juan's gas if he would drive us back down in his van. After a weed run or two, they suggested we *try* to see if the National Rainbow Gathering was still going on in Ocala, and if not, catch up with the next Gathering in Mississippi. Adrian had a real job and was out. I was in because even though I didn't really know what this was, I knew it would be an escape from what was certain to be doom, gloom and shame at my parents' house. They began to expound on the Rainbow Family and their gatherings, and I eventually fell asleep in the back seat.

When I pulled up at noon the next day, without having called, my father was livid. And *then* I had to explain what happened to the car, which was worse. "Was it worth it?" he wanted to know. I wasn't sure.

I mean we drove to a tropical Caribbean island! There was a drum circle of like thirty beautiful people, and I danced until I could feel and actually see atoms of energy. Outwardly I took full responsibility for what happened, apologizing up and down, but inwardly I couldn't help to think that maybe the outcome would have been different had there been more flexibility on their part. In the very least, I would have felt comfortable calling them about the car issue or giving them an update as to what time I would be home if they were more open and approachable. There is a famous quote, "Worrying is like praying for something you *don't* want to happen."[8] Maybe all their worrying and negativity around us going to Key West was the energetic cause of our car trouble? I knew better than to express this line of esoteric reasoning. It would get me nowhere. The damage was done. I apologized yet again, and I went to bed exhausted wondering how I would break the news to them about this next adventure.

Going back to Key West with no money whatsoever would be an opportunity to put my faith in the Universe and my ability to co-create to the ultimate test. There was a popular counterculture catch phrase at that time, which was "Jah Provides." This is a song lyric from the Bob Marley song, "Satisfy My Soul" which means Jah or God will provide for us, but it was also an expression used amongst the hippie community to explain why we needn't worry about material possessions, money or work. It was an acknowledgment that we trust in a higher power, *not the system*, to

---

[8] Robert Downey Jr.

provide our basic needs. This was a belief that I was now subscribed to, so it made sense to try it on completely.

I would be continuing my studies of universal law and hoped to prove my hypothesis (to myself *and* to my parents) that there was more than one way to do things in this world, and you didn't necessarily need money or a real job to be provided for. In the past, I had traveled with some money and a loose plan, but I was about to up the stakes. I would sleep in Juan's van at night but without any money. I would take my jewelry and jewelry making supplies to trade or sell and see what Jah would send.

Presenting a simplified version of the plan (without Rod selling weed) to my parents went over just as I thought it would. They did not share my excitement of putting my faith in the Universe to the test. They said they understood if I didn't want to live and work in Florida and preferred to live in California, but this was *not* normal, going off to sleep in a van with Juan and Rod who I had just met. On some level, I did wish that I could have just "got in line," going to school or getting a real job. It seemed like the easier thing to do for sure, but there was an underlying current flowing through me. It was a call to adventure that was impossible to ignore. This was non-negotiable. Staying at their house with no other friends and no job would be predictable, sterile and uneventful. I had an invitation to an entirely new experience. I had to go.

While Rod was swinging his product, I wandered the streets of Key West with my jewelry, stoned and absolutely happy and clear, open to any and all possibilities. I took in the colorful Caribbean

culture. Brightly painted wooden houses with people peddling their
bikes slowly while smiling, apparently on island time. At one point, I
happened upon another culture altogether in the neighborhood of
Bahama Village where the fishermen sat with buckets of their local
catch as women negotiated prices and people chattered with relaxed
familiarity.

Eventually, I settled on standing at a busy corner, displaying my
wares on my arm. If I sold just one of my simple crystal or hemp
macrame necklaces for six or ten dollars, I could eat for the day. I also
made intricate necklaces with tiny glass seed beads that were labor
intensive and worth more but regardless if I sold something or not, I
had faith that somehow everything would workout. As the streetlight
changed from green to red, cars and pedestrians sped by me in
countless cycles. I started to feel dizzy in this sea of people getting
carried away in the current of their lives. I felt like I was a sedentary
rock in this three dimensional rushing river. There was no time as
people hurried past me in fast forward, more concerned with the
future than their immediate surroundings. The only people who
noticed me were clearly living on the street as well and tuned into the
same frequency I was. I'd lock eyes with a young man in dirty, hole
ridden clothing carrying a backpack adorned with shoes and water jugs
that swayed as his dog pulled him on a leash. We would smile from
adjacent corners, acknowledging one another as if to say, "I know that
you, kind homeless sir, are also aware of the incredible miracle we are
living in as you create your own physical reality outside of the
constraints of society."

One woman finally broke this hypnotic spell for me. As a local store owner, she was angry at me for selling my jewelry on the street. Wagging her finger in my face, she told me that she paid a lot of money in rent and did not appreciate vagrants selling their wares free of the exorbitant overhead costs she had to bear. That was my cue which sent me in another direction to Sunset Pier where I had heard many vagrants *did* sell their wares. I set out my jewelry on a small black cloth and began to doodle in my journal. This was the vagabond city center where many of the people I had noticed on the street (young hippies, punks, street performers, misfits and addicts) all came together. Not everyone was here by choice, but it was clear that everyone was looking out for one another. Assuming I was sleeping on the street, I was briefed as to which parks were acceptable to sleep in as the cops were really cracking down everywhere. When I told them I was in a van, my new friends advised me to drive it off the island to the next Key because the police also regularly patrolled parked cars not allowing people to sleep in their vehicles. Many homeless do migrate to Key West in the winter because of the warm weather, but a "cheap" motel is over $200 a night there so legitimate tourists try to sleep in their vehicles as well.

I talked to an older man about the unfriendly encounter I had with the angry store owner, and he suggested I go to the municipal building and pay a small fee for a vendor's license so that I would not be hassled by the police. I shared the fact that I currently didn't have the twenty dollars for the vender's license. We talked for some time as my drawing continued to transform. I'll never know if he took pity on me or really did like what I drew, but he offered to pay me for my sketch. He gave me two dollars and we said our goodbyes shortly afterwards.

Once the sun had set, I found Juan and told him about my day, and that unfortunately, I hadn't earned much money for food. He suggested I go to the church for dinner where they feed the homeless twice a day. I felt guilty because this was not my intention. I didn't want to be voluntarily homeless and depending on the system or taking from others who were in greater need than myself. I also pointed out that I did have enough money to buy a loaf of bread or *something*. Juan reassured me that this was a privately funded kitchen and that he actually knew the woman who ran it. She was a friend of his who had been doing it for over ten years. He had donated money to this particular charity and volunteered his time with her so somehow he was transferring his meal karma onto me.

As I queued up in line, I was astonished to have the same gentlemen that had given me the two dollars sidle up behind me. He had told me about the soup kitchen, but I hadn't expected him to be there. Now the small amount he had given me went a lot further. I was being shown that it wasn't any of the busy business people that had helped me that day but someone who was actually in need himself and may have kindly given me all he had. Jah was providing me with a huge lesson about giving and virtues. The homeless are generally looked down upon by the general public. This was especially true in the 1990's. They were stigmatized as unsuccessful or not being contributing members of society, but this man had contributed more to me that day than any other of the fancy strangers I had come in contact with. Hard work had always been presented as a virtue in my family, but I am realizing now that it actually isn't. Generosity, like the generosity that this seemingly homeless man showed me *is* a virtue.

In the days that followed, I came to rely on my new misfit friends. We shared enlightening conversations, pertinent homeless information, and even food with one another. I realized that *nothing* is as it seems. That these "lowlifes" were actually diamonds in the rough, who had more integrity and cared about other people more than many of the "higher-ups" who looked down their noses at them. I also knew that I wanted this spirit of giving and sharing without judgement to stay with me and to somehow incorporate it into my everyday life.

It was probably fortunate for me that Jah was *not* providing me with packs of free cigarettes at this time. And though I could freeload them off my new friends in small quantities, I did recognize this would be a good time to quit. I had known for some time that my smoking cigarettes was ridiculous, especially when I was so healthy otherwise as a nature loving vegetarian who biked, hiked and even ran regularly. Being a smoker had run its course. In the past, cigarettes had helped me to identify as a rebel and to initiate me into that group of friends. But what had started as anti-system was somehow evolving, and I knew I was looking for a healthier lifestyle with more purpose. It made it easier to quit, being far away from my cigarette smoking friends who knew me well, and the fact that neither Rod or Juan smoked. I replaced cigarettes with smoking pot, going on walks or running if I really needed to cut through that feeling of agitation.

I heard the phrase, "Get a real job" more than once as people dodged by me on the sidewalk, and I dangled my jewelry for sale in their faces. I realized I was being judged by my vagabond appearance, and that it may have looked like I was choosing to spend money on weed or drugs instead of food. But truth be told, weed was free for me back at the van. One day, after I ducked in for a smoke with Juan and Rod, I headed back out to the street again and began to skip and sing along to the reggae disc Rod had loaned me. Eventually, my discman batteries died and with no money to buy more, I began straight singing. Super stoned, I started with Sugar Minot's lyrics I had just heard, "Herb a dis ah herbman hustling, bright an early in the morning,"[9] and then broke into a skipping meditation to Bob Marley's, "Thank you Lord for what you've done for me, Thank you Lord for what you're doing now, Thank you for every little thing…"[10] After a while, my own lyrics started coming through in a constant stream, "Hey sister sunlight, Living by the earth right, Moon lit so bright, You're mine, New height!" Though it was silly, I repeated this chorus like a mantra as I continued skipping down the sidewalk.

Rod had told us there was going to be live reggae later that night and that he knew the bouncer who would let us in. It turned out to be an open-air venue, and even though I could hear the music perfectly from outside of the chain link fence, it was nice to be inside dancing once Rod finally saw me and talked to his friend who let me in. The band was excellent with a full brass section. I was dancing outdoors

9 Sugar Minot, "Herbman Hustling", single, Black Roots, 1984,
10 Bob Marly & The Wailers, "Thank You Lord", single, Wail 'N Soul 'M, 1967, vinyl

and listening to live music as the full moon came rising up behind the audience. I had a deep sense of gratitude for this rich experience I was having with no money at all, when I heard *my* lyrics coming through the music. The same words that I had made up singing earlier that day were now being sung and played by this nine piece band!

As the song continued to play, I went running to find Rod and Juan, desperate to prove this to someone by singing along to the best of my ability. Screaming to them to be heard over the music I explained, "I WAS SINGING THIS EARLIER! THESE EXACT WORDS! THIS IS FUCKING CRAZY!" As it came around to the chorus again, I began to sing, "Hey sister sunlight, Living by the earth right, Moon lit so bright, You're mine, New height!" They looked surprised and confused that I *did* seem to know the lyrics by this completely unknown band. Seeing I no longer needed to convince them, I just enjoyed the rest of the song in pure ecstatic bliss, absorbing as much of this deja-vu-channeling-experience as I possibly could. I closed my eyes and imagined the energy of this beautifully loud reggae jazz sound and the magic of this experience incarnating into my very being, wanting it to reside there forever. *This* moment felt like why I had chosen to come on this particular adventure at all. It felt like my reward from Jah or the Universe (what I was being shown) for having turned off the exterior voices of my family and society and instead, listened to my inner voice, the voice that I now knew was tapping into something far greater than just mind-manifesting. For me, this was evidence that we were all connected to the same voice and the same source of information.

Many cultures have theorized that creativity or ideas come from somewhere outside of ourselves. Both Ancient Romans and Arabian folklore expressed the belief that *geniuses* or *jinns* (later *genies*) were thought to be guardians or spirits who guide, protect and could be credited for certain human talents or creative gifts. Interestingly enough, it morphed into the word *genius,* meaning an extremely intelligent person. Elizabeth Gilbert elaborates on this in her book *Big Magic: Creative Living Beyond Fear* wherein she explores the idea that creativity is a living thing trying to come through those of us who are receptive. Her theory is if you are unwilling to listen or invest the energy to see a particular idea through, it will look to be manifest in another vessel, artist, author, etc. Gilbert proposes this is why many times the same scientific discoveries are made on the other side of the globe in and around the same time.

At that time in my life, I had no way of knowing other people and whole cultures had explanations for where creativity comes from. Rod and Juan believed that I had channeled this song, but they couldn't begin to theorize as to how or why this happened. After reflecting on my own, I began to see creativity being of air, ether or the Father of Native American traditions, Father Sky. Up until that moment, I had always felt very connected to the Earth's systems or Mother, but now I pictured my channeling coming from invisible lines of communication in the sky which were part of a masculine energy or provider. I envisioned these like the delicate lines in drawings of constellations that connect the stars, only these lines came from Source and they reached down toward humanity offering inspiration, creative ideas, story*lines*, music lyrics, poetry, hypothesis, theories, and more. I imagined these were the same *lines* of communication we use to convey information as well, to send our prayers, our hopes, our dreams, questions, doubts, fears, gratitude, etc. *This* was the world wide web. Music had always elevated and guided me, so it made sense that while I was happy, high, skipping, and thanking and praising Jah, through song, I would be opening to channel and receive the same lyrics I would hear later that day.

This experience was mind blowing to say the least, and I began to explore what exactly I was tapping into. I began to read more so-called New Age books, which just like alternative medicine, if you spend any time thinking about this at all, you will realize it is not new nor alternative; rather, it is ancient wisdom that has been the norm for thousands of years. I was reading the *Celestine Prophecy*, and Juan gifted me a book by Depok Chopra who was the first author that I discovered writing about the types of experiences I was having by merging the science of quantum physics with consciousness and self-improvement. The discussions I was having were now expanding as well. These were the sorts of things I was talking about with this community of like-minded homeless people that I had found. They were drop outs, creatives, free-thinkers, philosophers, and less-is-more types, just like me.

My new friends understood and shared my connection to the Great Mother (Earth) and the Great Father (Sky), but this wasn't something I felt was "normal" or that I could discuss with my family. My parents did not see my carefree lifestyle as being spiritual at all. They saw it not as carefree, but as careless. Now as my journey became more devotional (to Mother Earth and Father Sky), it was becoming increasingly more difficult to relate to my actual parents' worries about material concerns and outcomes.

Chapter 8

No Risk, No Reward

I experienced a common phenomenon while on psychedelics that is referred to as ego dissolution. This is the realization that we are not our minds nor our physical bodies. It's the understanding that the physical body that we identify with as "me" is a temporary vessel for our spirits. When I was nineteen, the understanding that my soul is eternal was a prescription for utter recklessness. It gave me total freedom within this temporary body to go where the wind blows, hitch hike, and travel in a van with guys who were selling weed amongst my other regular exploits. I was back at my parents' house repacking for colder weather to attend the Rainbow Gatherings and do just that.

My parents (who were still extremely concerned about my physical safety) were beside themselves. "Who are these *Rainbow people?*" My mother wanted to know, assuming this was the cult they would finally lose me to. There was no googling this bunch, and it wasn't as if they were in the Encyclopedia Britannica, so I explained what I knew. By law anyone can camp on U.S. National Forest land for two weeks, so the Rainbow Family takes one week to set up a temporary community in the forest and then hosts the gathering during the second week. There is no money exchanged within the community. Volunteers build kitchens and feed everyone for free. There is a barter circle where people trade goods and services, and even stages set up for music and entertainment. The purpose of the gathering is a prayer for world peace. This was the first event I had ever heard of with such a pure objective, which was definitely in alignment with my hippie mentality. I couldn't see how anyone could find fault in a mission statement like world peace, but this was about the time the word selfish began to get thrown around.

According to my father, I had no concern for anyone else's feelings but my own. My sister's car was still broken down at the mechanics because of me, and I just continued doing whatever I pleased even though my mother was worried sick. Part of me *did* understand their desire for me to be safe, but I knew that I was. Even though I had only spent a few weeks with Juan and Rod, they were like brothers to me. I felt very safe traveling with them, protected even. I knew things could and would go wrong, but I also knew that I had a good head on my shoulders, and I was a great judge of character. I had just seen that the risk *was* worth the reward. I was learning about and being exposed to things I would have never seen from behind a desk or a minimum wage job down the street from my parent's house, but there couldn't have been a starker contrast to our perspectives.

In my mind, I was setting out on a magical sparkling fairy tale journey in search of a rainbow village in the forest. I was excited to experience this alternate reality the Rainbows had created, to see if it spoke to me or possibly my future in some way. In their minds, danger lurked around every corner, and I was one step away from becoming a statistic on the news. I wished with all my being that they could understand and actually trust my judgement, but nothing I was saying was convincing them that Juan, Rod or the Rainbow People were actually my peace-loving brothers and sisters. They couldn't imagine *how* or *why* such a thing would exist, much less that I would be safe there. That would have taken a lot of trust and intuition, which I was realizing was *not* part of our collective logical (mechanical even) operating system.

I knew I was damaging our relationship, and I *did* care. I wanted to please them, but I also knew nothing I was interested in was going to meet the expectations they had set for me. Preserving our relationship would mean giving up myself and the freedom that was teaching me so much about the world, which caused me to question who the selfish ones really were. *I* was supposedly selfish because I wasn't doing what **they** wanted me to do. In order to relieve their suffering, they preferred I quelch my inquisitive nature and adventurous spirit to live out the normal, ordinary life that they had imagined for me (doing what they wanted). So how was my pressing forward making unconventional decisions for **my life** any more selfish than them wanting me to just follow orders without any regard for what I truly wanted for myself?

They were blaming my dangerous and reckless behavior for their suffering, and yes, a part of me understood how scary that was for them. They just wanted me to be "safe" and "secure," but I was so removed from material desire at that point that there was a definite disconnect from that reality. What I saw, was that their attachment to physical outcomes and expectations was at the root of their suffering, not anything I was personally doing. I knew that our reactions or overreactions to any given situation are a choice and something we *do* have control of. I also knew that fear had completely taken them over, especially my mother, to the point that she had given up her autonomy and was unable to do anything but worry.

Many people believe that hate is not the opposite of love, but love's yang is actually fear. Fear, not hate, is what fuels racism, and what fuels war. Fear of the unknown, for our safety, of not being the best, or not having enough. Even if we don't believe in war or agree with it, the collective *has* agreed that we have to participate on some level by having nuclear weapons out of *fear* of being too vulnerable without. *Truth* is considered love's counterpart. My parents could not see that I was living my life from a place of love because I was not taking into account their feelings when deciding to move forward into the unknown. But I was being guided by the things I loved, and what I thought to be true. And by following my heart, I was living in alignment with my highest truth.

Our best decisions are made when they are based on truth and love. If we give in to fear and choose to live in what feels most comfortable or safe, we are not allowing ourselves an opportunity to grow. It was unfortunate that my parents couldn't see that, and that fear, the fear for my safety, the fear for my future, the fear of what our family or the neighbors might think was enabling their ability to trust. They were unable to trust my judgement or in a higher power that I would be okay, and that I was finding my own way in the world. Trust was too much to ask of them in that moment, especially when I was exhibiting what they considered "unacceptable behavior." It saddened me that I was unacceptable in their eyes, but changing their opinion of me was going to have to come from *them* and would require them to completely rethink their belief structure. Trusting and listening to my inner voice was something I wasn't able to compromise, so I continued packing and was only home for one night.

Chapter 9

Rainbow Gangster

When we arrived in Ocala at the site of one of the biggest, regional gatherings of the year, the stages and kitchens were gone and there was just a small crew still there cleaning up. The Rainbows aim to leave the forest cleaner than how they had found it. We helped pick up any last garbage, but their work was nearly done. In fact, they were moving on the following day. Juan was the oldest and most responsible of the three of us. He carried the role of both chauffeur and leader. He spoke to one of the volunteers at length and learned there was a grocery store promotion that would benefit us. Winn Dixie had announced they were offering a $1 credit to customers for every expired food item found within the store. So, if we were to go shopping just after midnight when all the dates had changed, paying particular attention to the bread and pre-packaged foods that were time sensitive, we could earn ourselves at least $20 store credit, which could be spent however we saw fit. Apparently, there had been a swarm of hippies in the Ocala Winn Dixies, so those particular stores were doing a better job of removing expired items. But this had helped the community kitchens to feed nearly 2,000 people (for free) who had gathered during the last week. He advised us to try other stores on our way to the next gathering in Mississippi, which inspired us to continue on that very day in order to arrive at an unsuspecting Winn Dixie just after midnight.

We presented two carts full of expired groceries explaining that we had wanted to buy a 25¢ pack of gum when we noticed so many out-of-date items. The cashier was beside herself, but we had over fifty dollars' worth of store credit. This was how Jah was now providing and how I was able to contribute to the common good by helping to supply our meals. Rod wanted to buy a six pack of beer with the money and Juan put his foot down. So began a heated brotherly discussion that had become commonplace. "Absolutely not! This money needs to be used for essential items and food," Juan pointed out, as well as the fact that the two of us didn't drink. Rod began to pout and rant, not agreeing with purchasing the cookware Juan had chosen or the pads and tampons he had very sweetly encouraged me to get for myself. In the end, Juan won out and the beer was put back. We slept in the van just outside of Tallahassee, Florida.

The following day we continued our journey traveling down a backroad in Alabama. This was my first time venturing into the South. Rod spoke to the local owners of the gas station where we were fueling up asking if they had seen any hippies to make sure we were on the right track. "Oh yeaaah!" They expressed with their twangy accents wanting to know, "Where ya'll comin' from," and, "Where ya'll goin'," having never seen anything like it. Rod was asking the questions while his short dreadlocks bobbed around in every direction dramatically flailing his arms about beneath a brightly colored tie-dyed t-shirt. But once his questions were answered, they stood there in uncomfortable silence, giving Juan a long hard look as he finished pumping the gas. I doubted they could see the *rainbow* in these two Latinos and a disheveled white girl. Juan, who we fondly called the Rainbow Gangster because of his hard gangster appearance and his L-O-V-E knuckles inner softness couldn't get out of there fast enough, and he chastised Rod for bringing any attention to ourselves at all as we drove away. Rod blew him off, but Juan remained serious reminding him where we were, the color of their skin, and what the general attitude was.

We knew we were getting closer when we began passing VW camper vans spattered in Grateful Dead stickers and converted school buses. The guys knew to look for a tower of stacked stones as an indication of where to turn off the main road. I loved it! We were on a modern day treasure hunt to find a rainbow village! Sure enough, we found one, and then another natural marker leading towards the gathering. We met an elder named Caterpillar who was a classic looking hippie with long hair and an open patchwork vest. As a veteran Rainbow of many years, he gave us a historical rundown on the Rainbow Family and his long-standing participation. He went off on a tangent, explaining that he was unable to attend the first official gathering in Colorado in 1972 and continued to rattle off subsequent years and locations noting his attendance or lack thereof. He also offered information about the ongoing "forest politics" informing us that the government was trying to outlaw Rainbow Gatherings. The

Forest Service was suing the Rainbow Family of Living Light (their official name). Caterpillar was fully charged now as he further explained, "For this reason the Rainbow Family will continue to have no official leaders or hierarchical structure! The First Amendment gives us the right to peaceably assemble on public land! There is no one individual they can sue. We are a family, a tribe, all together, all one!" With this deliberation, he pounded his decorated walking stick on the ground shaking the quartz crystals and feathers. I could have listened to this free lecture for hours as it covered so many of my interests (hippie history, social science, and new age esoterism) and sensed he would keep talking, but Juan interjected asking him for more specific directions, the real reason we had stopped.

Caterpillar pointed us in the direction of Welcome Home, the entrance of the gathering. Just outside was A-Camp, which some said stood for Alcohol/ics Camp and others said was Anarchist Camp. Either way, this is where the people who enjoy drinking stay, as alcohol is not permitted inside the gathering. As we rolled by, I noticed there were mostly RVs parked there and older folks who true to form, greeted us with a can of beer in one hand and a cigarette in the other. I was mesmerized by these people. They were the renegades of the renegades, people who preferred to stay on the fringe of the fringe, choosing their alcohol over the gathering. I presumed they were all regular fixtures that traveled with this caravanning event but chose not to conform to these non-conformists. We drove under the Welcome Home archway on the main road inside the National Forest excited to see firsthand what the Rainbows were creating and meet new folks.

The very first day, I met a pretty boy with feathers in his two long blonde braids parted down the middle of his head. He had some Rainbow name that I can't remember now but will refer to him as Cosmic Crabs because that's what he had recently had, unbeknownst to me. I slept with him in his tent that night, which was still very out of character for me, especially when he didn't have a condom, and I told him it was okay just to pull out. Afterwards, he broke the news to me that he had just gotten rid of crabs (or pubic lice), which according to him, "wasn't that bad" but was prevalent at the gathering. He rattled on, continuing to warn me about sleeping with people I didn't even know without using protection. He cautioned against more serious STDs in general, along with Staph Infection, which was common and very hard to get rid of there. He called me *Little Sister* and even though I sensed he meant well, I still felt moved to point out the irony of what he was saying and to defend myself.

I opened up to Crabs, telling him that historically I had been a prude when it came to actually having intercourse. I told him about my first sexual experience having been date rape, and the fact that I'd only slept with a few people since. It was really through him that I was trying to work through some of my sex issues; let down my barriers, loosen up, and gain more confidence and experience. As I thought back to my first sexual experience and how it had served to protect me, I also realized that it was probably the main reason why fear for my physical safety was not enough to keep me from traveling. I knew bad experiences could happen anywhere, even right in your family home, in fact we know most sexual abuse does occur there. There is no safety or security, just like there is no such thing as perfection. Life is perfectly imperfect and uncontrollable. All plans are subject to change, all lives are susceptible to total upheaval at any moment. Even the richest of the rich are not exempt from life's circumstances. We can choose what we believe will be comfort and safety all we like, but there is no guarantee that our retirement fund will still be there when it comes time or that we will ever see retirement.

I spent that night in Crab's tent, but the following day I was back in the van. I woke up the next morning to Juan staring at me all starry eyed.

"What?" I asked him.

"You look beautiful when you're asleep."

Oh Juan, not you too, I thought. We had a heart to heart about what a beautiful person I thought he was. Sadly, he expressed he knew I would never want to be with someone who looked like him and that he knew I was together with Crabs now. That was not the case (of the crabs) at all. I explained how grateful I was for his friendship and for him taking me under his wing. We had become very close in a short time, and I loved him like a brother. I had brought my parent's family tent that they no longer used that could sleep 6-8 people. I had thought it could serve as group housing if it rained or provide shelter for a cuddle puddle (a pile of hippies all snuggling together). I told Juan it might be better if I set up camp separately. I explained that I always felt more social on my own. Without anyone who knew me present I was uninhibited and felt free to express myself any way I chose. I thought this would lend to a more whimsical experience of the gathering. He understood and said he would still include me in their nightly Winn Dixie grocery trips.

During that week I talked to so many new people, I learned all kinds of Rainbow nuances. I offered up my jewelry as trade at the barter circle and received a beautiful deck of Motherpeace tarot cards. Everyone's personal belongings were safe there, which is something I had never experienced before. A backpack or purse could be left on the ground, in a public place, all day long or for *days* unattended and no one would touch it. This was part of a no ground score rule everyone abided by. Meaning, if you found something on the ground, you couldn't just pick it up and take it declaring, "Score!" Proper Rainbow etiquette was to hang what you found in a nearby tree and if it was still there in one week's time, *then* it was yours. I also learned about "Drainbows." This is a term used to describe a Rainbow who is not contributing to the group by donating their time, money, or energy to build structures, latrines, and water systems or to cook food in the community kitchens. They are a "drain" on the communal Rainbow system. I laughed out loud when I heard the word being casually thrown around to describe someone's general personality or mood as well. "He's *such* a Drainbow," one girl told me as a grumpy Rainbow walked away from a conversation with us. During the day I would visit the various kitchens with names like One Love or the Hydration Station to see what they were offering or to lend a hand. Juan committed to helping a kitchen for the week, and apart from one more Winn Dixie run, I barely saw Rod.

For sunset, everyone gathered around the fire pit at Main Circle bringing their own plate (or bowl) and utensils. A talking stick was passed around the large circle if people wanted to speak. All news and announcements were shared at this time and then the "Magic Hat" was passed around to take up a collection for kitchen and community needs. Then we would stand in the circle holding hands to pray and chant Om. After that, the people working in the kitchens would come with huge buckets and cauldrons of food to dish up. Dinner was followed with drumming, dancing, and Rainbow songs and chants, at least for those who didn't go back to A-Camp. The Granola Funk Theatre was a stage constructed in the forest where the musicians, jugglers, comedians, and poets hung, performed and supported one another.

One evening at Main Circle I had a cute young woman address me and ask if I was available to talk. After she confirmed that I was in Key West over New Year's she explained that she needed to apologize to me. She told me that historically she had harbored a lot of jealousy, and this was something she was currently trying to work through. She described her boyfriend who had been playing the flute that night in the Duvall Street drum circle and the fact that she was sure that he was attracted to me. By her account, she had caught him watching me various times throughout the night and apparently this had sparked a reoccurring argument between them. I was completely flabbergasted. I didn't remember having ever seen this woman in my life, much less her boyfriend, and she was apologizing to me! I had her describe him again, and to my surprise, I vaguely remembered him (or someone) playing the flute. But I recounted my beautiful, energetic rain experience on LSD to her in reassurance that her boyfriend was the furthest thing from my mind. She shook her head stating *she* was the issue, not whether there actually was some mutual attraction, "I mean so what if there was, neither one of you acted on it or broke any trust." She said that she realized if she wasn't able to stop fabricating problems out of jealousy it was going to cost her their relationship, which would not be the first time this had happened to her. Seeing me at the gathering was an affirmation for her that we were family, and she was being given an opportunity to grow by speaking to me. I was struck by this woman's brutal honesty, and though I wasn't sure if I would ever find the need to confess something like this to a total stranger, I admired her for it and the courage it took to heal this aspect of herself in this way. I gave her a big hug, thanking her for her honesty and wished them both the best.

It got so cold over the weekend there was far less of a turnout than the five to seven hundred attendees the Rainbow's had expected. I hadn't packed the right clothing for 40 degree weather, so it was hard to break away from the fire at night. I stayed drinking the hot tea that was offered until I absolutely needed to go to bed. I hurried back on the trail and curled up in my Alaskan sleeping bag, shivering with my teeth chattering. It was too cold to take my many layers of clothes off to put on something that resembled pajamas. I also had to pee, but that would mean leaving the sleeping bag and taking off my sweatshirt in order to undue my railroad overalls, which I couldn't imagine either. I finally drifted off to sleep, relaxing my bladder and yep, I woke up to a very warm sensation as I was wetting the bed. Now I was forced outside into the cold. While bathing in the freezing river the next day, I learned another Rainbow nuance when I was severely scolded by a man who yelled at me, telling me not to use soap in any body of water, *ever*. I was beginning to see that Rainbow culture had their own set of rules and regulations as well as people who delivered them in a variety of ways.

There was a lot of beauty and magic in this alternative community. Some people were full time Rainbows who lived nomadically, traveling from one gathering to the next, completely avoiding "Babylon System." Others just went to a few gatherings per year when they were able or one annual gathering. Of course, it takes rain to make a rainbow, and I also saw there were a few dark clouds that went along with the gatherings. Living minimally outdoors had led to lack of personal hygiene and self-care amongst many of the diehards. Volunteers dug latrines at every gathering and provided potable water for people to drink, but without money for soap, shampoo, antiseptic, medicine, etc., bathing and general health care went by the wayside for some. I saw that everything Crabs had warned me about was true, especially the rampant head lice. In fact, my own head was beginning to itch.

I shared the same ideology as the Rainbows; a commitment to non-violence, to healing the planet and living in harmony with *all* our brothers and sisters regardless of race, religion, class, gender, etc. Some of the Rainbows were environmental lawyers or had other careers that allowed them to take this work out into the world, but this like-minded group was mainly living within the bubble of their intentional community. I admired their effort to live a life closer to Earth and reduce their environmental footprint, but I found myself asking just how much coming together to raise our vibration does actually do for the planet if we don't step out and take that intention into the world at large?

As Caterpillar had explained, there was no one leader of the Rainbow Family, though with so many people gathering in the forest, it did take a lot of organization; therefore, there were organizers and some guidelines (or rules) for things to run smoothly. This was a beautiful path, but I knew it wasn't mine. Finding a ride to the next Gathering would have been easy, but this mobile utopian society was not my truth. Like the A-Campers, I was too much of a non-conformist. I could see what I was craving included more personal freedom and self-purpose. Besides, my return flight to California was coming up in just a few days. I had a ride back to Miami with Juan to get me there just in time.

Upon my return, my parents were happy to see I was alive, and I was bubbling with the details of the gathering. My dad loves the outdoors. In fact, growing up, our family vacations were usually camping and fishing trips. He had been following the weather in the news. "Weren't you cold?" He asked dubiously.

"Yes," I rattled on about layering and less attendance. Then, I shared the sheer genius of the Winn Dixie scam.

"I didn't raise you to be like that," Mom said, expressing her disappointment as she examined my head for lice, which, sure enough, I did have. I ended that visit lying on their cement patio in the backyard, soaking my head in the dog's bowl full of lice medication. Mom picked the dead gnats and eggs out of my hair, as she worried aloud that I may be spreading them to California friends or on my flight the following day. She was always doing her best and *trying* to have a nurturing relationship with me, but in the end, I knew it had to be on her terms. My parents' motto was, "My way, or the highway," and I was becoming numb to their totalitarianism, worry and disappointment. I refused to let it suck my shine. As she continued to comb and pull on my hair, I wriggled around in the chair and happily sang, "I'm going back to Cali, Cali, Cali, I'm going back to Calim, hmmmm, I don't think so."[11]

---

[11] LL Cool J, "Going Back to Cali", single from Less Than Zero, Def Jam, 1988, vinyl and CD

Chapter 10

Traveling Weed Saleswoman

I landed in the small airport of Ontario, California near where I had grown up and spent time with close friends there. None of these friends were in college full (or even part) time. They were busy with decent paying jobs and their lives, and I still had no real intentions of working in that moment. I put my feelers out to see if anyone was interested in returning to Alaska with me to sell marijuana over the summer, but it was met with no reception at all. The general consensus was that it was too risky, especially when they all had legal income streams they could depend on. I moved on to visit friends in Chico, thinking someone would be up for this adventure during their summer break from school. Feeling like Holding was still one of my closest friends, he was one of the first people I spoke with, picking up our conversation (and my intrigue) where we had left off the previous fall. As I was telling him once again just how lucrative the marijuana market was in rural Alaska, I was surprised when he began to add momentum and direction to my loose vision. All I knew was that I wanted to return to Alaska to sell weed and to somehow see more of this beautiful state. He pointed out that by flying to Petersburg we would be limiting ourselves to one island and suggested we broaden our horizons by instead purchasing a plane ticket to mainland Alaska. Then we could travel the summer bluegrass music festival circuit I had described to him before. There would obviously be a built-in customer base at these events, so the idea was brilliant. I was elated! I couldn't have thought of a better plan myself. Soon after our conversation, he had gathered a team and was developing a business plan.

Our close friends, Sue and Gino were keen to join us. Sue was a fair skinned strawberry blonde environmental science major who had lots of wilderness experience. Gino was a classic looking Italian-American with a thick head of shoulder length black hair who always had a five o'clock shadow. He wore nerdy glasses that deflected the assumption that he was a pot dealer, though he kind of was. But the best part of all of this was that they were a couple, which I thought may lend to Holding and I finally becoming one as well. I saw my window of romantic opportunity and suggested he and I share a tent to keep our backpack weight to a minimum.

The plan was simple. Now that I was back in California, I had access to my parents' refunded college money that was still sitting in my California savings account untouched. This account had no corresponding atm card or bank branches in Florida, hence the savings. I would invest nearly all of this money, approximately $1,400 which would probably make me the largest shareholder in this joint venture. The others would try to gather as much money as they could between now and then to put all of our money together and buy as much weed as possible. We would keep our expenses to a minimum by traveling the state camping and hitch hiking. We could divide all of our earnings on a percentage basis that would reflect each person's initial investment. It was a seamless plan, one whose earning potential would provide me with enough money to pay back my parents *and* get myself to Costa Rica for the winter (now the seasonal nomadic lifestyle I was envisioning for myself). This is how I justified spending my parents' college savings on marijuana.

We agreed on our dates and plane tickets were purchased. Then we set about allocating tasks to one another to ensure our mission would be carried out successfully. Gino would be in charge of purchasing the weed since he had the best connections. Sue was organizing our staging grounds in the town of Valdez where we had mutual friends working as nannies for the summer. Holding being the eternal Boy Scout would handle outdoor gear, maps, camp stove, cookware and cutlery. I was in charge of logistical operations which entailed gathering intel on the Alaskan music festival circuit, so we knew where we had to be when. This required talking to Eva who had left the fish cannery work early last summer to travel the state according to their bluegrass festival schedule. And then I just had to show up for my flight. With my only assignment being a phone call to Eva, I ventured off on a side trip, hitch hiking to Colorado to visit a girlfriend, and I was unaware of how dramatically our plan had changed until we arrived in Valdez, Alaska.

We landed in Anchorage late June, and I vaguely remember all of us staying the night in someone's shitty city apartment where we smoked lots of ceremonial weed to consecrate our adventure. Not the weed that we would be selling. Gino was too paranoid to fly with that. Our product was being shipped to headquarters in Valdez. The two girls we all knew from Chico State had hooked us up with this place to stay in the city and a five hour car ride with their friend to the small coastal town of Valdez the following day. As I curled up in my sleeping bag on the dirty beige carpeting, everything seemed to be falling into place.

Our minds were blown as we left Anchorage, driving through mountain ranges along rivers, lakes and a glacier. As we winded southwest on the Richardson Highway, we paralleled the green snaking Alaskan oil pipeline. We had a ride as far as the Tsaina Lodge that overlooked Thompson Pass where our driver and new friend would work for the summer. His co-workers were happy to show us around and share stories of the famously harsh winters here that made it such a badass destination. At that time, this area hosted an annual World Extreme Skiing Championship, which was a helicopter assisted event, meaning helicopters dropped competitors off on a remote mountaintop that they would ski down. There were tall beacons, approximately six meters in height all along the highway to mark the road and aid in snow removal. This means the road had the potential to be lost beneath six meters, or eighteen feet of snow, making it the area of Alaska that receives the most snow in the entire state.

As we sat sipping hot chocolate, someone offered us a ride into town, and soon we began our descent through Keystone Canyon which included beautiful roadside waterfalls, lush green ferns and colorful splashes of wild flowers. If that wasn't impressive enough, the winding highway finally gave way to views of Prince William Sound with its small Valdez Harbor, which was surrounded by dense green forest. I couldn't imagine how the people living and working in the small dots of houses and businesses below got through their mundane tasks of daily life. It seemed absurd to be indoors with the incredible beauty of the ocean, mountains, glaciers, waterfalls and streams all around them. This was validation that I was doing the right thing for myself. I was giving myself the time and opportunity (which I may never have again) to explore this beautiful nature and culture. Later, those same inhabitants pointed out that I was witnessing *one* sunny summer day, and they reminded me that they also experience lots of rain and long dark winters as well. Regardless, the natural beauty of Valdez has stayed with me as it is definitely one of the most beautiful places I have ever been.

My friends seemed to have me, and me alone, on a need-to-know basis regarding our game plan. It could have been my lack of a home and phone number, my carefree personality or the fact that I was the majority shareholder, but everyone except me seemed to know the following details. Our friends, the girls we were staying with, were nannying for a married couple, both doctors. Doctors who were also into wilderness guiding for large groups, so they had an entire basement filled with outdoor equipment and bunk beds where we were welcome to stay. Gino had sent our weed disguised in a care package to the *doctors' P.O. Box*! These were professional people that had a family who I was sure did *not* smoke weed. I was upset by the fact that they had decided to send illegal substances to these unsuspecting professional people's address, but the next piece of information that they shared was far worse. In fact, they cringed as they told me. What we would be receiving at the doctors' P.O. Box was two pounds of shwag or Mexican grown brick weed. This was a *huge* deviation from the plan because typically no one wants to smoke or purchase this low low-quality weed, and two pounds was *a lot* of it.

Apparently, Gino had panicked, unable to find the dank weed we all knew and loved (a common problem in 1996) and didn't want to risk arriving empty handed. The first I heard of all this was while Gino was at the post office, and we were nervously waiting, hoping and praying he would return with our package. We breathed a sigh of relief when he arrived smiling, care package in hand, shwag weed packed in jars of peanut butter. In the evening we walked this Alaskan neighborhood, smoking whole joints to ourselves until we all had headaches and had reached a decision. It wasn't our intention to put the doctors at risk. We would head for the hills the following day. The nannies had told us there was a trail nearby where we could cross a river and hike to a glacier. Team Regs would camp there a night or two and then head out on the ferry. Holding had been studying his map and was happily planning our route to the music festivals which was time sensitive and dependent on the success rate of four people hitch hiking together.

In the morning we set out towards the glacier. The trail was a cinch, but the river crossing was definitely more complicated than I had expected. It was fast moving glacial water, heavy with silt thigh deep. I was about done there, especially after Holding demonstrated his field knowledge warning us of the higher risk of death here, not only because of the water's temperature, but the heavy silt itself which can quickly weigh you down filling your clothes. Everyone refused my idea to hold hands to get across, reason being, if one went down, we all went down. Last to cross, they threw me a rope instead and I begrudgingly made my way in the shockingly cold, icy water, my toes and feet completely exposed in Teva sandals. The snow was nearly finished melting in the mountains, so they reassured me there could only be less water upon our return.

We regrouped, changing into warm socks and shoes as planned and then continued to hike until the glacier came into view at the head of the valley. The glacier itself reminded me of a stern, protective father overseeing the entire valley. It actually had what looked like a heart shape of black earth showing in the center where it was melting. It occurred to me that this could be symbolism for not only Great Spirit loving and protecting us on our journey, but possibly a reminder that my own father's rigidity actually *does* come from a place of love. We made camp with a view of the glacier and the river nearby. Everyone set to work pitching tents, gathering firewood, taking in the beautiful scenery, wildflowers, and mushrooms. Mushrooms that the boys swore were psilocybin or magic mushrooms. They bruised purple, so we all began harvesting as many as we could to dry, and then possibly sell. We *mostly* agreed (three to one) that someone should test their potency, in small quantities, knowing the dangers of poisonous mushrooms. Sue was outnumbered, and became angry as the three of us tried just a few small shrooms each.

I began to feel a little something in my stomach as I often did with magic mushrooms, but I was already high on nature and marijuana, so I wasn't sure if they were actually psychedelic or slightly poisonous and affecting my stomach. I honestly couldn't back the legitimacy of this new product 100%. This was our first campfire dinner conversation. The boys swore they thought they were psilocybin and Sue voiced her serious concern about selling unidentified mushrooms that could potentially harm someone. Holding retorted with a reasonable compromise saying, "We'll just tell whoever we sell them to that we found them ourselves so to be really careful," he added his cute little bobble head shrug thing I loved, as if to say that was that, no-big-deal, meeting adjourned. Getting nowhere, Sue went to bed mad, and we enjoyed the rest of our evening glacier viewing on our marijuana and *maybe* a mushroom buzz under the midnight sun. Our first night in the tent together, I tried to gauge Holding and our potential relationship status. "So, are you tired?" I asked. "Do you think you feel the mushrooms?"

"Good night, Miller," was all I got, as he turned his back away from me.

The mushrooms slightly altered our travel plans. We now needed to stay one more night at the doctor's before we left on the ferry to give us more time in civilization to sell our new product.

Sure enough, as we had pizza and burgers at a local town restaurant, we met some young people who were interested in buying a big Ziplock bag full of discounted magic mushrooms. Holding pitched the sale to them and then left us girls to small talk with our customers as the guys ran back to the doctors' to get the shrooms. We shared the fact that we were selling weed at the Alaskan summer music festivals and that the Talkeetna Bluegrass Festival, a notorious biker blowout, would be the grand finale of our summer extravaganza together. They mentioned that they hoped to go to Talkeetna as well. The exchange was made, $130 for well over an ounce, and in saying goodbye they mentioned, "Maybe we will see you in Talkeetna." Holding reprimanded us for sharing our future whereabouts with people who we may or may not have just sold bunk magic mushrooms to. Sue, now our voice of reason, quickly retorted, "We shouldn't have even been selling them in the first place."

Holding ended the conversation with, "Are you kidding me, that's a killer deal for them," smiling and head bobbing with his adorable shaggy look.

We left Valdez via the Whittier ferry, which I proclaimed a *Poor Man's Cruise Ship*. The boat paused to watch whales breaching with the incredible Otter Pop blue Whittier Glacier in the background. We saw a plethora of sea otters and puffin birds all just by public transportation. "See, who needs to pay for an expensive cruise?" I asked.

We were headed to the Girdwood Forest Fair, which also involved a train ride. As we waited for the train and chatted with some other festival looking folks, our first pot deal was made. This was a huge relief, providing hope that our plan still might actually work even with this shitty marijuana. Holding recorded the sale and set the money aside.

Once we arrived in Girdwood, we found the perfect place to camp in the forest just outside of town. It was a campsite that had been used many times before, complete with a fire pit and a few makeshift wooden benches. Our first morning there, I opted for some alone time as the "kids" (what we fondly called one another) went to explore and try their luck salmon fishing in the nearby river. Things became quiet as I began to write and draw in my journal. So quiet, that I thought to look around, quite possibly sensing someone or *something* wandering into our camp. I spotted a black bear cub coming in nose first, smelling the air with inquisitive, short sniffs where traces of our wild blueberry oatmeal breakfast possibly still lingered. It continued to explore the benches and chairs right across the fire pit from me with its nose where we had all just sat to eat. *And your mother?* is the first thought that popped into my head. I began to move and hum softly to let him know I was there. When that didn't seem to change his course much, I told him, "This is our camp," a little more sternly. This prompted a pause, a few more sniffs, and then he continued on in the direction he was headed, as if to say he could have things his way. My heart was beating fast as my eyes searched for mama bear, who I hoped I would *not* encounter. I began singing and shuffling nervously around camp, cleaning up and checking there were no remnants of food. When it seemed the coast was clear and the cub was alone, I became excited that I now had a bear story to share with the others!

When they were headed back, they were clambering so loudly, I could hear them from quite a long distance away. "Guys, guys, we had a bear cub in camp!" I exclaimed.

"WE KNOOWWW! There's bears EVERYWHERE!" they declared. Gino was so animated, so it was easy to put my story aside to hear all of their morning excitement. He continued rapidly, "Sue got right between one and my salmon, throwin' her hands up like she was a bear herself! You should a' seen it Miller. There were so many salmon in the river. I stabbed one with your knife and it started getting away. We followed the knife upstream throwing rocks, and finally the hatchet. Sorry we lost your knife to that fish, but then I caught another fish with my bare hands!" Gino began jumping and throwing his hands around reenacting how he had caught and thrown the fish down on the ground yelling, "Whatcha gunna' do now that you're on LandddddDDD mother fucker!" Clearly, I had missed out.

"So, my dead grandfather's knife is gone, correct?" I asked truly upset, not knowing how they could have let that happen.

"Yeah, sorry Miller, but you should have been there! We saw four bears! They were there in the dumpster and fishing in the river!"

"Sue, you *know* you shouldn't get between bears and their food," I said now taking my turn as the concerned one in the group. To which Gino responded, "That was MY food," still wound up, jumping all around. They agreed that those bears were from another world and boundaries were definitely in order, but in the end, the bear had won because they had seen the need to walk away, leaving him their potential salmon dinner.

There was about twenty hours of daylight now. We were enjoying art at the festival during the day and music in the evenings, but thoughts of bears made the nights seem endless to me. I had a hard time sleeping knowing just how many bears were around. We were hanging our food, but tent walls were not a reassuring barrier for me. I had multiple visions of a bear ripping into our tent at night. In fact, that's mostly what I laid there focusing on all night long. At one point I put my arm around Holding, possibly for some comfort or maybe just as an inquiry to see if things could deepen between us. His honest-to-God reaction was, "Miller, stay on your side." I was shut down as if we were fighting siblings. He drew an imaginary line between us in the middle of the tent. Like his pesky little sister my response was, "But whyyyy?" We had a few rounds of "because" and "because why," and then he told me to leave him alone and go to sleep. "I'm scared of the bears," got no sympathy, just empty reassurance that nothing was going to happen. At least this gave me something else to think about. *Why wasn't I allowed to cross the imaginary line? We both really care about each other and there is a mutual attraction, I know there is.*

As our journey continued, our days were determined by the rides we were given. Four people hitch hiking isn't an easy task. It took a lot of faith on the driver's behalf to trust a bunch of long-haired hippie kids enough to allow us all into their vehicle. We were determined to stick together if at all possible, but if we had to separate, it was to be done by tents and couples. Not that Holding and I were an actual couple, as he had established that, but a male and female who shared two sides of a tent. We decided to split up food and cookware as well. In the event of a lengthy separation, each pair would be self-sufficient until we eventually met up at the next festival. Many times, we would stand roadside for hours; smoking, laughing, then getting serious again. Gino and Holding would consult the map to see if there were any camp worthy points of interest nearby where we could stay in the event that we did not get a ride. This would then get a rise out of me, telling them to, "Think positive!" I had begun to realize that *believing* is seeing, and not the other way around. It was when I elevated and aligned my energy with the Divine, embodying what I wanted to manifest, that my circumstances aligned as well. Confident that we would get a ride once everyone's attitudes changed, I'd sing something from my Bob Marley repertoire, "Positive vibration, Yeah! Positive! Say you just can't live that negative way, If you know what I mean, Make way for the positive day… Are you pickin' up now?"[12] I'd add, "Are you pickin' *us* up nowowow?" Aiming my question at a passing car. They'd roll their eyes, but a car would slow down and we would all gather our packs and run to find out the details of where we could possibly be going to next.

Together we explored the Kenai Peninsula, camping amongst the cannery workers, selling them weed. We also ventured to the artistic town of Homer, sleeping at a hillside neighborhood

---

[12] Bob Marley & The Wailers, "Positive Vibration", Track #1 on Rastaman Vibration, Island Records, 1976, vinyl

campground. Sue and I ended up exploring the Homer Spit on our own. This natural tourist attraction is a 4.5 mile long glacial spit that juts out into Kachemak Bay. The local boat harbor is there as well as a number of hotels, bars and shops. There are tents scattered along the beach in multiple campgrounds where transient workers live. We enjoyed looking at art, browsing the gift shops, meeting fellow travelers, and selling weed for the first time on our own. We noticed the Orthodox Russians there who dressed similarly to the Amish but drove big, shiny, new four-wheel drive pickup trucks.

As we were hitch hiking our way back to our campsite, two Russian women in a huge brand new truck slowed and rolled down their window for us. This was my first interaction with people from this traditional looking culture and their scarf covered heads and long old-fashioned dresses piqued my curiosity. In my mind, I envisioned Ewok type houses in the trees, and I couldn't help but to blurt out with my thumb still in the air, "Take me to your village," truly wanting to know more about how these people lived. The women both laughed, and the passenger told us that they weren't going very far. Still, I thought out loud, "I want to see where you live and what you do." They let us climb in but reassured us that their community wasn't that great of a mystery. "Just some houses and farmland." I insisted we wanted to see it, knowing it would be a worthy detour, but they let us out on the highway as they turned in to the supermarket parking lot.

I wish I could say we spent more time in the Denali National Park at Mt. McKinley, but we just spent one night in one of the roadside campgrounds. I still have a visceral memory of walking along the trail because as we did, a giant grizzly bear with a collar crossed the path in front of us. Holding whirled around so fast yelling, "BEAR" while throwing his arms up in the air that he backhanded me in the face. "Uggghhhh, I saw it," I snapped, holding my hand to my sure-to-be-bruised cheekbone. When we arrived at the ranger station to check in and pay, the bear was all the buzz. We learned he had a collar and tracking device on because he was a problematic bear. Generally, they will follow and record these bears' activity, and after repeated offences, be it raiding the garbage, tents, cars, or aggression, they will airlift the bear far away with its collar on. If the bear finds its way back, it may have to be relocated again or possibly destroyed. Problematic bears were not good bedtime stories for me, and Holding wasn't letting his guard down. Even though he felt horrible for hitting me in the face, and that did result in an immediate hug and apology, it wasn't gaining me any relationship headway.

One particular day we were standing alongside of the Denali Highway in front of Miller's Mini Mart and Ice Cream Shop. It must have been seeing my own name and the magic of this serendipitous moment that inspired me and only me to drop acid alongside of the road while we were still trying to hitch hike. The ingestion was met with head wagging and tongue clicking, which I took to mean this wasn't the time or the place. But for me, clearly it was. It was "Miller Time" and as I started feeling it coming on, this became a big part of my trip. It was time for me to take acid because the Miller Store was right across the street. All signs were pointing to yes, the Miller sign, as I repeatedly pointed out. Holding looked at his watch again and sighed while rolling his eyes, letting us all know that we had officially been in one place for more than three hours. This was the longest we had ever waited for a ride. According to him, all signs were pointing to it being my fault for being high on LSD and carrying on like a whack job on the side of the road. Someone suggested we get some Miller ice creams to break up the wait. I wasn't allowed to go into the store, but I do remember eating my vanilla double decker swirl cone while we continued to hitch hike from across the street. Eating would be an understatement. I made love to that ice cream cone, taking in all its sweet creamy goodness, its coolness, its flavor and texture. Time was irrelevant. Why did we need to get anywhere? Why were we in a hurry to leave this beautiful location in front of the Miller's Ice Cream Store? As all the stars were coming into alignment and the clarity of the ice cream cosmos was shone onto me, in that perfect moment of time and space, someone finally stopped to give us a ride. It wasn't far, but it got us away from the beautiful store traffic and closer to the town of Healy and the Anderson Music Festival, or the *Mother Earth* Music Festival.

Ironically, up until I had thrown my wallet into the forest, the kids had been referring to me as *Moneybags Miller*. This was because when we would hold fireside accounting sessions, as the largest shareholder, I would receive 65% of all our earnings from this horribly seedy brown marijuana, but this was not a fortune by any means. Even though we had been plugging away and sales were fairly regular, overall, our business endeavor was proving to be less lucrative than we had originally thought. Aside from the quality, we deduce that the quantity we ourselves were consuming and what we were allotting to trade, mostly for better marijuana and other drugs, were the cause for the reduction in our profit margin. I estimated that the night I spent communing with Mother Earth at the Anderson Music Festival, I must of had about three hundred dollars (or five hundred at most) from nearly two months' worth of sales when I threw my wallet into the forest.

That next morning, as I showed my friends where I thought my wallet could have landed, I agreed that yes, they could keep all the cash if they found it. As they continued searching with no luck, I spent most of that afternoon zonked out in my sleeping bag, unconcerned. My wallet also contained my California driver's license, but that had been revoked, so other than it being my only form of personal identification, it really didn't serve an actual purpose anymore. I still had a trickle of income with our weed sales and had also lost $200 in traveler's checks, which I could try to reclaim. It wasn't the material items that mattered to me; it was the actual experience that night in the Alaskan wilderness that had seemed very real and highly relevant. In fact, in the time since I've wondered if like Stanislav Grof's (one of the godfathers of psychedelic research and transpersonal psychology) work suggests, psychedelics do "have the capacity … to exteriorize otherwise invisible phenomenon[13]," making what I saw in the forest entirely

---

[13] Stanislav Grof. *Realms of the Human Unconscious: Observations from LSD Research*, Souvenir Press, 1975

possible. It's not that I think that Mother Earth really was that dying tree, but I do believe the waves of energy I saw emanating from nature and becoming the air we breathe *is* probably the actual exchange we have with each breath, and psychedelics enabled me to see that. I also believe that when I saw the Earth's demise in fast forward, that is absolutely what is happening to this planet. What I was experiencing during so-called hallucinations seemed more than plausible and far more exciting than the limited collective reality that we have been told is our only reality. We've been told that "what we can see with our own eyes" or what we can prove scientifically is the only thing that actually exists, but here I was seeing all of this with my own eyes, which prompted me to ask *who's to say what is real?* However, I knew these things were better left unspoken, so *I* wasn't the one to say much about it at that time. Now as we traveled through this physical reality, I would stop at a payphone and call the 1-800 number for my traveler's checks that I claimed had been stolen.

The rumors of the Talkeetna Bluegrass Festival being a biker drug fest didn't disappoint. This was a three-day festival on private property with an eclectic mix of attendees; musicians, bikers, drag queens, drag queen bikers, hippies, and families both young and old. We made more friends, sold some weed, and I dropped more acid spending lots of time on my own. The first night, I approached a group of Alaskan guys about my age who were camped near us sitting in a small circle on some logs talking, drinking and smoking. They laughed as I offered to sell them some weed, and judging by their attitudes, I gathered that they *were the weed*. They were from Matanuska Valley, where the infamous marijuana strain, the Matanuska Thunder Fuck originated. They became egoic as they bragged about the high quality weed they were growing, which was beginning to feel awkward. The nicest and cutest in the group, Jimmy, introduced himself and his friends to me, telling them to chill out. I sat and we shared one of their potent homegrown joints and some conversation. I gave them a brief synopsis of my summer and explained that this was the last weekend I would share together with my friends who would be returning to California shortly. I told them I was planning on staying in Alaska and continuing to travel on my own. Jimmy was the most interested and engaged. He asked where I was planning on going, and I think we were both surprised to hear me say, "Cost Rica." It seemed like a long shot now with my shwaggy financial situation. He invited me to stay in the cabin he was building which was theoretically, "on the way to Costa Rica" since it was located on the Al-Can highway. He told me that he lived off of Route 1 which passes through Alaska and then continues on to Canada, the U.S. and Latin America, all the way to the tip of Argentina. Though not my usual hippie-type (Jimmy was dressed in a black leather jacket full of silver zippers as well as worn out black jeans and some kind of death rock black t-shirt), he was cute in a blonde rocker kind of way, and I knew that Alaskans were an unusual bunch. He told me that his friends were growing weed out there and that they all played music together. He suggested that I come by. I tucked the directions he wrote down for me away in my pocket.

The second night I got back to the tent late but Holding was still up, and we smoked a friendship bowl together. Sue had finally explained his relationship reluctancy to me. She told me that he had been heartbroken the first time I left for Alaska, and then when I returned but didn't stay. He hadn't wanted to initiate a relationship with me only to have me leave again, and he also didn't want to stand in the way of my free-spirited lifestyle. I knew this was partly true, that a relationship may not have kept me there long term, but I also wished he would have communicated this to me last fall. I realized that part of me had been looking for more stability through him, and maybe I would have stayed *back then* if he had reciprocated my affection, but that was neither here nor there, not now. Nothing about living in California was calling to me anymore. I had begun to understand and relent. My giving up seemed to have made things more comfortable and even closer between us.

Holding told me that they had run into the kids we had sold the mushrooms to back in Valdez. They were super angry and said they had been looking for us. They were demanding their money back because the mushrooms hadn't worked at all. He was obviously concerned, becoming more worked up as he rehashed his interaction with them. He described his response as one of surprise telling them, "That's strange, the mushrooms worked for us." He told me we clearly had to adopt a no-refund policy as none of us could afford to pay them back. My friends had managed to get away without paying them anything, but he advised me to "lay low" for a while. If they did spot me, he warned me not to return immediately to our campsite, giving up our location. Great! He had obviously put a lot of thought into this. These people didn't know where we were, but having just smoked, I became extremely paranoid. I lay there replaying all the possible violent scenarios that could potentially go down with the mushroom people in my mind. They were coming for us with axes, with knives and physically pulling us out of our tents. Sometime in the early morning, I finally fell asleep.

It was a party all night, sleep all day, repeat kind of weekend for me. I managed to steer clear of the mushroom people and was up all night on a mellow dose of LSD the last night of the festival. As I walked back to camp through the muddy parking lot, out of the mist of the early morning, a group of biker drag queens appeared, like an apparition. Teetering on high heels, they hiked up their skirts and dresses to mount their bikes, trikes and sidecars. Their motors rumbled to a start but strangely enough they just drove a short distance and then performed what I can only describe as a biker-drag-queen-fire-drill. Everyone dismounted, ran in circles, wobbling once again, hiking up sequined skirts and pink tutus in order to plop down on a different motorcycle or in another side car. Moments later the procession began filing out of the muddy parking lot, engines revving, bespattering mud as they disappeared into the fog; long beards, jean jackets, flowing skirts and all, myself as the only witness. It was the perfect encore for a perfect summer because even though we hadn't made the money we had anticipated, at least we had done it! I felt a huge sense of pride and accomplishment for the four of us having thrown caution to the wind like this. I knew this was a trip of a lifetime, something people wait their entire working lives to do in an RV when they retire, but we had seized the moment, realized the time was now, and just went for it! This was *exactly* the spirit that I wanted to continue living in, not waiting for some far off future plan to feel alive or make my dreams come true, but to do the things that make my heart sing in the present moment.

Later that day, the kids were going to make their way back to Anchorage. Everyone felt bad leaving me on my own and asked if I wouldn't reconsider and fly back to California with them. But I was happy to stay there, and besides, it would take nearly all of my money to buy a plane ticket. There really wasn't anything waiting for me there now. I had just spent an amazing two months with the people I cared about most. And to the contrary, *I* felt sorry for *them* having to leave such an epic adventure to return to school. I knew that if they were lucky, they might spend a summer abroad before a long thirty-some year career began for them. I was committed to my spontaneous-happy-and-free-trajectory. I'd throw the dice and see what else Alaska had in store for me.

Chapter 11

$3 Cabin

I stayed on to recover and help clean up a few days after the festival. The owner of the property where the festival was held and a crew of trusted bikers and boozers were there, so it felt like a fairly safe environment for me to ease into being on my own. I really had no idea of where I was headed next. I opened my journal and pulled out the directions to Jimmy's that he had written on a small piece of scrap paper. Would that be my next destination? But on my way to where? Costa Rica? With my budget, this was probably a pipe dream at this point. Back to California by land? As the only woman on the cleanup crew, my new friends were asking where I was headed and invited me to leave with them hitch hiking all together, the seven of us. When I showed them the tiny piece of paper where I *might* be going, they confirmed that we would all be headed in the same direction. I could hitch with them as far as Wasilla and then they would continue south, and I, east. Knowing I couldn't stay camped out at the festival grounds forever, I agreed and acknowledged that the wind was now beginning to blow me in this new direction.

Jimmy had given me a phone number, a landmark and the mile marker of where to find him but not knowing what day, time, or if my plans would change, I hadn't bothered to let him know I was coming. When I arrived at his landmark, the AK Mountain Lodge, the elderly woman there who was presumably the owner looked annoyed that I wasn't a guest-to-be. Instead of helping me to locate who was seemingly her neighbor, she just pointed me to the payphone to call for myself. Jimmy wasn't there, but I spoke to his friend who helped to move the message along that some girl (I) was at the Mountain Lodge waiting for him. Before long, a car came skidding into the gravel driveway and Jimmy hopped out, saying a quick goodbye to his buddies before they sped off again. We exchanged a long hug and he helped me with my backpack, carrying it directly across the highway to his friend's property. His childlike excitement was contagious as he began to show me around, pointing out and naming the surrounding mountain peaks and telling me how happy he was that I was there.

As we put my backpack inside his small cabin that was still under construction, I realized Jimmy was the outward expression of everything I was discovering, but not articulating, multiplied by ten. Whereas I was still trying to "act normal" and blend into mainstream society when necessary (at the bank, grocery store, in conversations with strangers, etc.), I could see he was loud and proud. Everything about him exuberated anti-establishment, anti-excess, anti-waste, anti-war, pro peace, love, marijuana and music. He had trumped the system, building his cabin himself with all recycled materials. He boasted that he had salvaged the wood and the windows, and a friend had given him the small wood burning stove for heat. His only investment was $3 on nails when he had gone through most of the old rusty ones he could straighten. Being a musician, he related living in the present moment to music. He found when he and his friends played completely improvisational music that was when "the magic happened" and they created some of their best "organic sounds," which could never be replicated again. It was also the beauty of being present and absorbing each moment versus getting distracted by trying to hold onto any one thing. Jimmy didn't have a traditional job. He played music, helped his friends grow and sell their weed, and was focused on finishing his cabin before winter. We passed his friend's real home as we walked to the back of the property which overlooked the wide Matanuska riverbed. He told me he referred to himself as a "positive nuisance," because he was aware that his extremely good energy annoyed most people. He laughed at the ridiculousness of people preferring to remain grumpy and unhappy instead of jumping on his positivity train.

His friends and property mates were the complete opposite. Wyatt was obviously generous, letting Jimmy build a cabin on his land. He was actually good looking with longish brown hair and a well-kept beard, but he and his girlfriend Bailey were the stereotypical Alaskans; a strange hippie/redneck/renegade breed that mainly just wanted to live out at the end of the road and be left alone. They loved nature, weed, ATVs and their guns. They spent most of their time on the couch, watching television or playing video games in sweatpants and tie-dyed or metal band t-shirts with their firearms close by. Occasionally Jimmy would talk them into playing music. He'd play guitar, Wyatt bass, and Bailey played the drums. They would hardly leave their property to drive the twenty-some miles to the grocery store, much less go to Anchorage or out of the state. Bailey had stringy blonde hair, and though small, was tom-boy tough and swore like a sailor. She would occasionally *try* to talk to me, but other than smoking pot, we had nothing in common. Wyatt immediately tuned into my California, vegetarian tree-hugger vibe and set about trying to shock and offend me. At the mention of both Jimmy and my vegetarianism he would pipe in, "I love animals too, cute little furry ones. I love to kill them." They both used the N word and would cock their guns when their emotions ran high usually while watching the news or at the sight of any squirrels in the yard. Jimmy would brush them off by laughing and telling them, "Put that shit away."

Jimmy invited me to stay and help him finish his cabin. I expressed hesitation mentioning I still wanted to make my way to Costa Rica, as well as my inability to tolerate his horribly behaved friends. He advised me to not pay them too much attention stating, "They are good people at heart." I begged to differ as trigger happy racists did not fall under the good people category in my book. In the childish stoner voice that he often used, he told me, "Don't let them get you down, girlllll. Always be happy, be high, spreadin' good vibes sisterrrr." Instead, I made a conscious choice to *positively* try to keep to myself and to rely on and engage with Jimmy's anarchist friends as little as possible. And I think the feeling was mutual. I didn't get any warm fuzzy vibes from them either. In fact, I had never seen their underground grow operation, and I got the impression that they really didn't trust me.

Regardless, Jimmy and I began to fall into a familiar rhythm together quite quickly. We spent our days exploring the riverbed, finishing up the construction, gathering wood for the stove or doing tarot readings. It became my job to pound out any last recyclable nails and to gather leaves in garbage bags to insulate the cabin for winter. There was no indoor plumbing, just a spicket outside so we would cook simple meals on the wood stove, but I'd have to go inside Wyatt and Bailey's at least once a day to poo and for an occasional bath or shower. I would break this up by paying for showers and laundry at the neighboring lodge from time to time. Jimmy tried to encourage a relationship between his friends and I, coming to get me when the bong was being loaded, a good movie was about to be watched, or live music played. Occasionally I would partake, but mostly I spent my time alone, protecting my personal energy and doing what brought me joy; reading, beading, drawing, writing, and now meditation. Jimmy taught me the vibrational sound for each of the chakras and with much coaxing, I would join him in sitting and chanting while we meditated together. It began to feel comfortable and safe being with him, and before long I found myself in a somewhat healthy and enjoyable sexual relationship. We were talking about the future, which for me, never included winter in Alaska.

Periodically we would hitch hike to Jimmy's family's home just ten miles down the road, but we were so far out on the highway, in full autumn, sometimes only a few cars would pass in *hours* so we would have to give up and call it a day. At one point, Jimmy wished it *was* winter because then people would *have* to pick us up by law. He tells me that in the state of Alaska, it's illegal to leave a hitch hiker on the side of the road during winter. A fun fact but still no reason for this California sunworshipper who is already freezing her ass off in September to live through an extreme Alaskan winter. On the days we did arrive, Jimmy's dad, stepmom and two half-sisters provide a welcome break from the cabin with Wyatt and Bailey. We would usually spend a few days with them, staying in a real house that didn't require waking up and going downstairs to restock the wood stove in the middle of the night. We would use their real kitchen and would try to carpool to town with them for more supplies.

Jimmy was vegan and after much mooing while I ate my granola with cow's milk, I surrendered to veganism as well. This was mostly due to social pressure, but I did know that he was right, that if I truly cared about the inhumane treatment of animals, then I shouldn't support large-scale dairy farming. His whole family hunted and judging by the family photos in between elk heads and mounted animals, it looked like Jimmy used to hunt as well. I noticed several versions of a younger Jimmy on the wall with big blonde curls and sparkling blue eyes. In some, he's in a bright orange hunting vest posing with family members and a rifle in his hands. In others, he's on one knee, holding the head of a dead animal, smiling, his fair skin rosy from the cold. When I asked him about it, he would shut down, telling me that was something he *used* to do before he knew any better and his younger brother went to jail. He said that now he realizes it was too violent.

I learned more about what it is to be a true Alaskan from Jimmy's family. Unlike Wyatt, Jim Senior took an educational approach when talking to me about eating wild game and hunting. He explained that most hunters do actually have a deep connection with nature and the animals they harvest, sometimes spending days at a time in the forest, studying them and their behavior. And that historically, man has always hunted, helping to keep animal populations in balance. "Now, we have the Department of Fish and Game to manage what percentage of wildlife can be harvested to protect, and to be sure that certain species aren't overpopulated." He impressed upon us both that it's natural meat, no antibiotics, no crowded mass farming, always offering up a taste of whatever they were cooking, be it moose meat, deer burgers or caribou sausage. Jimmy refused to even use their meat pans to cook our vegetables, which for me, was entirely unnecessary. Not only did I not care if their pans had been used to cook meat, I could see that his loud and proud anti-establishment approach was off-putting and hurtful to the people in his life who viewed things differently.

His family was extremely tolerant of Jimmy's (and my) lifestyle. His father owned his own electrician business and in between contracts he was home cooking, relaxing, reading novels, and watching movies with Jimmy's young half-sisters. His stepmom took care of the girls and all their animals. In comparison to my always busy, highly productive parents, they were both very relaxed. Dishes would be piled up along with the laundry or a number of chores, but everyone would be curled up under a blanket, staying warm, sipping hot chocolate, engrossed in a book or a movie plot. This slower pace felt extraordinarily comfortable to me. It made me realize that my parent's drive and the need to be productive had always made me feel like I should be busy doing something as well. It felt like utter indulgence and acceptance, to be able to sleep in and allow things to "just be" as they are.

Jimmy's dad gave up on encouraging him to come to work for him as an electrician and started working on me, explaining what a good opportunity it was for him. All this talk about work gave Jimmy another idea. We should venture to Kodiak Island where his dad's electrician business was based. Not for him to rough-in houses, but to sell Wyatt's weed that was nearly ready for market. He said it would be a good way for me to see the island if he *was* going to work there someday, maybe once we got back from Costa Rica. Before I knew it, we were overnighting in Anchorage with Jimmy's musician friends and then hitch hiking back through familiar territory on the Seward Highway to catch the ferry. Once in Kodiak, we camped for free at Gibson Cove near the smelly fish meal plant with a quarter pound of (though not the Thunder Fuck) excellent Matanuska grown weed. Jimmy had been to the island a number of times and knew enough pot smokers that the weed was spoken for very quickly. He also knew where the good dumpsters were behind the big commercial grocery store. Jimmy climbed up and picked through what would normally be astronomically expensive imported produce. There were whole boxes of good apples set alongside one dumpster and loaves of seeded multigrain bread. Any doubts I had about eating from a dumpster were quickly replaced by Jimmy's enthusiasm and my agreeance with his for-the-people rhetoric. "These big companies are connected to the machineeee, girllll, they haveeeee to throw out all this perfect goodnessssss to make room for the new, like a factory. Do you get what I'm sayinnnn?" I got him, and I shared his sense of triumph. These were riches most people couldn't afford, like a slew of seven dollar imported pineapples, now free for the taking. It was a bag-lady-abundance-from-excess kind of moment with Jimmy standing on the top of the dumpster beaming, holding pineapples over his head like trophies.

We took one day to sightsee. Jimmy wanted me to see fossil beach, where yes, there are fossils, and there is also a surf break and a huge heard of buffalo that we were fortunate to drive slowly through. It was over an hour away, but we hitch hiked there and enjoyed our day combing a beautiful stretch of beach and searching for fossils along the shale cliffs. We picnicked and played throwing our driftwood canes into the strong wind seeing how far they would be carried. We were feeling high off of our weed and the beauty of our natural surroundings, where this wild forest meets the frigid sea. The ride that we managed to catch on our way back, however, was a very sobering experience. Sobering for us, but not for them, as we quickly discovered that the two men who picked us up were way too drunk to be driving, especially on the steep cliffside roads that wound around numerous bays back towards Kodiak town.

It started out as a normal hitch hiking experience. We got in and introduced ourselves, but Jimmy's presentation of me as his girlfriend sparked something inside the passenger. He was now turned around in his seat yelling, slurring, and pointing his finger, oscillating it between both of us as we took turns getting yelled at. He demanded to know why we were only boyfriend and girlfriend. He yelled at Jimmy asking, "Don't you want to take this woman to be your lawfully wedded wife?" He continued on, leading us through a loud, accusatory wedding ceremony as the driver swerved, laughed and added his own nonsense. It was obvious these men were not going to intentionally harm us, but their driving could. And it seemed like that was about to happen when the driver floored the gas. We both screamed for them to stop the car and let us out. They laughed in their drunkenness, but when we continued to demand they stop and they saw we were absolutely serious, something (in at least the passenger) clicked. He told the driver to relax using, "They are our friends," to convince him to drive like a somewhat normal human being. "And no matter what you two do, if you get married or not, that's all right with me, okay. You're my friends. You got that?" We did, and we thanked them when we made it back to our campsite alive. In all of my years of using alternative transportation, I can thankfully say that was actually the worst experience I have ever had.

It was nice to see Kodiak Island, but it was a six hour drive (if you had a car, which we didn't) and then a twelve hour ferry to get there. It wasn't cost effective or safe to continue to do the same run regularly. As a small community, I imagined it would only be a matter of time before people realized what we were up to. Still, I liked the fact that there was a town. If we lived here, we could easily walk to the grocery store, restaurants and social events which were things that were all missing for me way out the road, with no transportation at the cabin. And about that cabin; It wasn't so much the $3 cabin, as it was the cold and Jimmy's friends when I told him I just couldn't spend the winter there. I knew we realistically didn't have the money to go to Mexico or Central America, but that's the only thing I had envisioned for my near future. And staying true to my vision, I convinced him we should see if we couldn't go into Mexico or at least Guatemala. Before long, we had a rough plan.

Though we'd be squished, four to the backseat, Jimmy talked his parents into letting us drive down to the lower forty-eight with them on their annual trip to spend Thanksgiving at his grandma's house in Idaho. We could continue on to Latin America by land via Jimmy's mom's house in Arizona. I had obtained an Alaskan ID card, and we were applying for our first passports, which without thinking about, I had worn my embroidered marijuana leaf Planet Earth t-shirt for my photo. The passport lady thought it might be a problem, but it turned out to be undecipherable and the perfect way to reintroduce myself into the system, with a great big hidden marijuana leaf up-yours kind of message in my picture. I spoke with my Southern California friends and learned that one of my favorite couples in our family of friends would be traveling from Eastern Washington very close to Jimmy's family, all down the coast back to where I had grown up. We said goodbye to the cabin and Wyatt and Bailey, and soon enough, we were traveling with members of my peace-loving tribe, camping out of their truck. Harmony was one of my best friends. A sickly sweet, beyond beautiful girl with long locks who loved to smoke *ganj*, even more than her handsome boyfriend Damian, also my good friend. She had recently finished a one year healing arts program at the HeartWood Institute in Northern California, which piqued my curiosity.

Along our journey, we stayed at a Nazarite community in Eugene, Oregon where Harmony's girlfriend was living. These outwardly hippie looking folks were high(ly) devotional, having taken a number of Nazarite vows extracted from the Old Testament or the Torah (the first five books of the Hebrew Bible). They abstained from wine or anything "of the vine" including grapes, grape juice and raisins. They vowed to not cut their hair, letting their dreadlocks grow long as an outward symbol of their devotion to

God. They were also forbidden to be near any corpses, even dead family members. Somehow, somewhere they had also worked smoking an incredible amount of high grade marijuana into their doctrine, and there was a whole lotta *chalice* being smoked as everyone busily prepared for Shabbat. It was crunch time, as all the cooking, cleaning and regular chores needed to be completed before sunset Friday which commenced their complete day of rest, family time and communion with God.

As we passed from Atara's (the Hebrew name Harmony's friend has been given) living quarters to the main house, we were greeted with, "Shalom Shalom," by multiple dread heads bowing with their hands in prayer. Being absolutely gorgeous also seemed to be a prerequisite for indoctrination into this community. Curious to learn more, I asked questions as we smoked from the chalice, mostly about the Sabbath. They described the challah bread that was being baked as we spoke, the lighting of candles and prayers that would be recited. Feeling a bit uncomfortable as an outsider and by their level of stress, I pointed out that theoretically I could keep working after sunset and asked if there was anything I could do to help. "Absolutely not," was the response from one incredibly sexy disciple. "No one can work. This time is strictly for rest and worship." But, being pre-Shabbat, he took me up on my offer and put me to work washing the dishes.

I hadn't eaten very much that day and the heat of the house was all rushing towards me and out the only open window above the kitchen sink. It actually felt like all their energy was rushing towards me, as everyone's eyes were fixated on me washing dishes as they continued to smoke and chat. I felt the intensity of both the weed and the Nazarites' focus peaking as my knees went weak and I lost consciousness. I woke up on the kitchen floor to Jimmy hovering over me, super concerned. Later, when the four of us discussed all the factors of this incident; my low blood sugar, the crippling weed and seclusive energy of this group of people, we diagnosed it "normal under present circumstances." This helped me initiate an overdue and embarrassing conversation about meals and the fact that it seemed I needed to eat more, and more often than the rest of them. I confessed that I had routinely found myself hungry, light-headed and headachy before the other three even thought to begin preparing meals. Damian was super supportive about my dietary needs and was the only one to admit that he didn't really like the vibe there, suggesting we leave first thing the following morning to not interfere with their Shabbat. I didn't feel comfortable here either. The community energy was very strict and felt strange to me, so I quickly voted in favor of leaving but backed down when an argument ensued because Harmony wanted to spend more time with her friend, and Damian was sure this was a cult. Harmony spoke to Atara and, Shalom Shalom hooray, we would be leaving the next day. We would shove off to visit another Diva in Harmony's circle of friends who was studying nurse midwifery.

The Nazarites had inspired Jimmy to become feral and he began to encourage me to grow dreadlocks with him. I became intrigued by talk of alternative careers; midwifery, massage therapy, and acupuncture. Harmony was glowing when she talked about her experience at the Heartwood Institute and she and her friend chattered about the offerings at the nearby Oregon College of Oriental Medicine. I ask more about Acupuncture which would be interesting, if it wasn't a four year commitment that consisted of difficult medical studies. Her friend shared that her midwifery curriculum was hard, too, and the girls continued to buzz with excitement about home birth babies and alternative healthcare. I agreed that dreadlocks were about all I could commit to in that moment, and Jimmy and I stopped brushing our hair. He was more influenced by Rastafarianism and I certainly resonated with thanking Jah, eating Ital foods, and always preferred to smoke ganja over drinking alcohol. But for me, dreads were less about Haile Selassie and more of a back-to-nature statement, as Bob sang, "Resisting against the system," or as Jimmy always called it, the *shit-stem*.[14] Harmony and Damien agreed to stay one night in Chico, as it was in route and would give me an opportunity to see my friends. By the time we arrived there, I had a massive bed head that Jimmy was helping me with by rolling the large nappy sections into round dreads with his hands.

I had given Sue a heads up we were coming, and I saw the whole gang, including Holding, but I found it to be very uncomfortable introducing him to Jimmy. "So how did you two meet? At the Talkeetna Bluegrass Festival?" he asked in what sounded like a half hurt, half forced older brother tone as he assessed the situation. I couldn't help but to think that things could have been very different if he would have reciprocated during any one of my attempts at affection. Luckily, he had just dropped by to say hi, and the next day we were back on the road headed to

---

[14] Bob Marley, "One Drop", Track #7 on *Survival*, Island Records/Tuff Gong, 1979, vinyl

Jocelyn's house, my best friend who was now living near Reno, Nevada.

Damian and Harmony only stayed one night here, but I wanted more time together with Joce and her longtime boyfriend, who was also a dear friend of mine. So, we stayed on, opting to continue by means of hitching later. We saw a great concert (GLove with Dave Matthew Band), gathered wild sage in the desert, and quartz crystals. We visited the herb shop and made some tinctures and natural remedies. We cooked up lots of healthy food and did a ton of beadwork together. At times, I was embarrassed by Jimmy's unfiltered authenticity because even though I would understand and agree with the things he expressed, it was too much, and other people had no idea what he was talking about. Babylon falling, Mother Earth School or thought creation were topics he commonly expounded on. Friends (even *his* family and friends) would become uncomfortable and look to me for a more intelligible translation. I'd try to drop it, but Jimmy unafraid to speak his truth, would go on to poetically explain the cosmos and thought creation as he understood it. "It's like an idea born, a ganja seed that goes on to make a beautiful plant, that you can smoke, like ganja weed." He truly was a light beam ahead of his time that most people just rolled their eyes at, not knowing how to respond to him.

Eventually, Jocelyn drove us to a junction in the middle of the desert where we could continue on hitch hiking to Jimmy's mom's in Arizona. As we got out of the car and said our goodbyes, the wind picked up. Jocelyn was hesitant to drop us off as we were now in a full sandstorm, literally being pelted by sand. However, there was no going backwards, as Jimmy's father had told us many times, "Onwards and upwards." We had to crouch down with our hoods and jackets over our faces and ears which was not the best position for moving onwards. Someone did take pity on us though, and before too long, we heard honking and saw headlights flashing so we ventured out into the sand and then inside a large green Cadillac.

Chapter 12

The World

Our plan was to cross the border into Mexico from Arizona where Jimmy's mother, Shannon lived. Shannon had moved from her home in Idaho to be closer to her youngest son and Jimmy's only full brother Robert. The longer Jimmy and I were together, the more Robert's story and how it had affected Jimmy's life change gradually began to unfold. Robert had been tried and convicted as an adult in the state of Alaska for second degree murder when in fact, he was seventeen at the time he committed this crime. When he was first arrested, he had been held at the Palmer Correctional Facility in Alaska just down the road from his father, stepmother and four siblings before his trial. It was easy for his immediate family, his girlfriend and young son to visit him there. He was eventually sentenced to twenty-one years with the possibility of parole in seven and relocated to a privately owned, medium security prison in the state of Arizona where he knew no one. This enterprise needs to import its customers, and this could have been the reason for him being tried as an adult when he was in fact a minor. Their entire business model is financially incentivized by crime continuing to be committed and harsh sentencing for any and all offenses. Robert's incarceration 3,500 miles away from his friends and family prompted their mother to quit her job and move her life to an entirely new part of the country.

Robert had taken the life of another teen during a relatively routine drug deal. The victim was black, making it look to be a hate crime. Jimmy and I both agreed that calling this senseless act a bad decision was a major understatement, *especially* for the family of the boy who was killed. He and Robert had grown up very close, being only one year apart. They knew all the same people, but Jimmy had a different mindset and a small group of close musician friends he hung out and jammed with. Before Robert "fell" (the term used in prison to describe when an inmate mis stepped or committed their crime) he and Jimmy had enjoyed the same Alaskan activities; hunting, fishing and target shooting practice. Robert's crime is what sparked Jimmy's veganism and his strong opposition to guns, which as many people who were close to him routinely pointed out, did not involve a gun, but a knife. Regardless, this is what had led Jimmy deeper into the hippie counterculture of peace and love and is why he now refused to play violent video games or Dungeons & Dragons, which all his friends still loved.

Shannon, a recovering addict, worked on the Gila River Indian Reservation as an addiction counselor as well as a caretaker for infants and young children of troubled parents. She had started a new life for herself drug and alcohol free and was living with her boyfriend, Walter. She had met Walter in Arizona. He was a prison warden at yet another privately owned and operated facility (Arizona is bustling with them). Shannon was beautiful. She wore her wide curls in medium length graying blonde hair. Her age and cigarette smoking were slightly more pronounced in the wrinkles around her mouth, and her wrists jangled with all her Southwestern turquoise jewelry. She was kind, clear, and creative, making stained glass art in their tiny extra bedroom. I was drawn to her creativity, crazy life experiences, and endless conversation. She and I fell in love immediately.

She had this counselor, empowering, but not enabling thing going. In fact, I was mesmerized by her communication skills. She made it clear she was happy to have us there, but that we couldn't stay very long in their small apartment. She suggested if we wanted to stay through Christmas, which *had* been our plan, that we rent a cheap apartment or trailer nearby. This was quite surprising for me, coming from a family where my parents had just spent months questioning me about whether or not I was coming home for the holidays. It made sense though that a recovering addict and a prison warden wouldn't want two pot smoking hippie kids staying in their tiny apartment for who-knows-how-long.

Together, the three of us began to discuss possible plans and our financial situation or lack thereof. Shannon listened well and offered up ideas that supported what we wanted to do. It felt less like parenting and more like figuring out the near future with a friend who had way more life experience than us. In fact, she openly admitted that she herself had made so many of the wrong choices, having "seen and done everything," that even if we went to Mexico with no money at all, it probably wasn't possible for us to screw up our lives to the degree that she had in her lowest moments.

She continued to ask us questions and offer suggestions to help us make a decision that felt right for us. At one point, she mentioned if we found work in that area and stayed for just a few months we could save more money for our trip and Jimmy could spend more time with Robert. This was something we hadn't even considered. Now we were faced with the question of whether to hurry up and head over the border (with my heart set on a tropical adventure, I voted for the original plan) or to stay, not only to earn some travel money, but also so Jimmy could spend more time with his mom and brother, something he hadn't done in years. As the discussion became more circular and uncertain, she suggested we all go to visit Robert together before making any decisions.

On our first visitation day, our dreadlocks and unconventional clothing threw up immediate red flags. It was obvious they did not want to let Jimmy or I through security to see Robert. I was wearing a long, baggy, hippie dress that Harmony had sewn which laced up the back. It looked like a calico potato sack, and could only be considered sexy in this situation, if you've been in jail for years. But they were trying to deny both of us entry. Shannon stepped in and calmly explained that we had come all the way from Alaska to visit Jimmy's brother, Robert. She clarified that there was nothing wrong with Jimmy's attire and kindly asked that he be allowed to see his brother. There was a bit of a debate over Jimmy's hair which Shannon pointed out that *he* was not an inmate and could wear his hair in any style he pleased. I would have to wait outside which Shannon apologized to me for, saying she hadn't thought about my dress because she herself always wore jeans or slacks.

Even though I hadn't met Robert that first day, I completely understood Jimmy wanting to see his brother more than twice while we were in Arizona. He had shared with Robert that we were considering staying, which of course had gotten his hopes up. It now boiled down to one week not being enough time, and a few months possibly being too much (at least for me), but I did acknowledge that we lacked a plan and any budget at all for going to Mexico and Central America. When we had shoved off from Alaska, we didn't really know how we were going to make this trip a reality, but now Shannon was offering a viable solution. When she found us a little trailer for $175 a month and said she would help by paying the deposit, that sealed our new deal. We moved into a trailer park with mostly Mexican residents which was "perfecto" because it gave us an opportunity to practice our Spanish. As a conversation starter, and possibly to keep ourselves accountable, now we would tell everyone we met in the trailer park that we were traveling to Mexico soon. We began filling out job applications to stay and work a few months before we crossed the border.

From this point forward, Shannon would loan us her car to venture to the prison on our own. As she herself said, she was there to provide regular support for Robert but was sure he would appreciate time alone with us young people. During our visits, Jimmy would fill him in on old friends and news from home. They would get to laughing over memories of the stupid shit they used to all do together. We would also paint a picture for him of our temporary life in Casa Grande and our plans to travel to Central America. Robert was an artist and was learning to do tattoo work. He would describe the makeshift tattoo guns he'd secretly build late at night in his cell, or the fermentation process of orange juice which was the only alcohol he had drank in over a year. Occasionally he would bring his drawings to visitation to show us his work or pull another inmate aside who would roll up a sleeve of his gray jumpsuit to reveal a tattoo Robert had done. His personal drawings were on the dark side; grim reaper and demon type of things, but always with impeccable detail using a fine point black marker pen. In contrast, Jimmy and I were all hearts and rainbows.

At times Robert would go into short anti-imprisonment rants stating it would be better if we all took the law into our own hands. "Kill them all and let God sort them out!" On these occasions, Jimmy would miraculously turn into a responsible older brother, becoming uneasy. He would warn him against any trouble, be it an angry mindset or contraband. "You gotta' get outta' this cage, Bro. You gotta' get out on parole. Remember peace and love and stay out of trouble, man." If things became too serious, Robert would change the subject by pointing out that we only had an hour left together. We would then tell him more about us, about the outside, and our days in between visits.

For Christmas Jimmy gave me my dream trike, a three-wheel bicycle with a wide basket in the back. This was to help get me to and from my job at Quizno's sandwich shop. Yeah, dream bike, not job, but I was willing to make this short term sacrifice to see our long term goal through. We had Robert cracking up as we described how this old bike's steering wheel was sticky and had a strong pull to the right. When I first rode it, I was getting pulled around in circles to where I couldn't stop or peddle straight. It pulled me right into a light post, making me leery of riding it the two miles to work.

As much as we shared with Robert, there was always a slight disconnect, at least for me. Besides our obvious differences, I sensed that he *was* a white supremacist and probably understood our desire to go to Mexico and veganism even less than I related to what his life was like behind bars. Regardless, I realized that this is what *unconditional support* looks like. We were all fully present for each other and providing support, even if we didn't approve of or fully understand one another's choices, appreciating the little time we had together.

When Jimmy finally found work, it was just for a few days moving empty boxes after Christmas, and it was becoming more evident that we were basically saving money from my minimum wage job to travel to Mexico indefinitely. He felt terrible about not contributing, but the Universe was giving him more time alone with Robert. He reminded me about the Alaskan wages he could earn with his dad on Kodiak Island, swearing he would be the one to work for us both when we got back.

It had been my first Christmas away from home, so my mom took it upon herself to come to Arizona for a visit. I knew she was coming to check up on me, and was *not* going to approve of what she saw. She came at the end of January, staying at a nearby hotel for a long weekend and just as I suspected, it was a lot for her to swallow. I was living in a tiny twenty-four foot trailer, with dreadlocks; Jimmy was being his radical love light musician self; his brother was in jail; and we were preparing to travel into Mexico and Central America with no real plans or destination. She had a stunned look on her face much of the time as she tried to digest what Jimmy was saying, and we shared some of our favorite pastimes in the trailer with her. He played guitar and I played my new talking drum he had encouraged me to buy for our trip. We cooked food as we listened to the classic records we had checked out from the library; Woodie & Arlo Guthrie, Captain Beefheart and his Magic Band, and Miles Davis. She took us out to eat and met Shannon, commenting on how nice she was to move her life to Arizona for Robert. All and all, I think it went somewhat well. There were no tears, arguments or unsolicited advice.

As we transitioned into the month of February, I became more proactive with preparing for our trip. We borrowed Shannon's car to get our vaccinations, and I came home with a few outdated Mexico travel guide books from the library. At night I would read excerpts out loud. One book read something like, "If you find yourself in the uncomfortable situation of having to use the bathroom outdoors in a public place, you can create more privacy for yourself by closing your eyes." What a piece of advice! We laughed so hard we cried. This helped to release some of the growing pressure of disapproval that was building up all around us.

I had shared our plans with a Mexican co-worker I was close to, and his first response was, "You're going to get yourself killed." Then my dad called (yes, we had a landline in our trailer) to talk with me about our lack of planning and faulty sense of reality. He had worked in newspaper plants in many of the major cities in Latin America and knew from experience that everything was not "all good" there. It was poor and dangerous, and we really didn't know what we were getting ourselves into being on buses and trains. I absolutely believed him and reassured him we were not aiming to visit the industrial areas of the major cities that he had seen. Our plan was to travel the coast, the ruins, lakes, and temples, avoiding capital cities when at all possible. That may have shined a little crack of peripheral light into his perspective, but again there was no room for a discussion. He made it clear he could not support our decision to travel to Latin America in this way.

Both of these interactions had shaken me up. We were standing on the precipice of the great unknown, preparing to jump into our first planless *international* adventure. It was true, that we *didn't* really know what we were getting ourselves into, but that was the appeal for us. This was going to be another culture, and a completely new experience. There was not going to be any hotel reservations made, and aside from the Pacific Coast, there was not going to be a destination chosen. We were going to camp and go wherever the wind blew. I was used to my parents' general disapproval, but this time, it felt like a bomb had gone off, and that bomb had blown open a space for doubt to creep into *my* psyche. I don't recall if my dad had actually said they would not help us if something went wrong, but by the end of the conversation, it felt a whole lot like the phrase he used all during my childhood, usually when my sister and I started out roughhousing and laughing, "Don't come crying to me when somebody gets hurt."

I wished they could offer me the type of unconditional support we had been sharing with Robert. I wished they were able to love and support me regardless of if they agreed with or understood my lifestyle. Their complete objection began to get under my skin, and I started questioning my own judgement. *Were we going to get ourselves killed? Could my dad be right and possibly have more insight than us? Will we be putting ourselves in serious danger?* And then, *wait a minute, has he even ridden a bus or train in Mexico? Maybe we should just rethink our mode of operation, save more money or have an actual plan?* After days of torment, I asked Jimmy what he thought we should do; if we should go, cancel, or postpone our plans.

Jimmy suggested we ask the Motherpeace tarot cards, so I brought out my deck. Repeating different versions of the same question in my head, my hands hovered over the deck. *What should we do in the matter of traveling to Central America? Should we travel to Central America? Should we travel to Mexico? Should we travel at all?* I slowly drew one card, and turning it over, the *World* card revealed itself. In the center, it featured a colorful, hand drawn African woman dancing. She's pictured holding a burning torch in one hand and a tambourine drum in the other, surrounded by naked women of all races. They were touching, supporting and holding one another in a circle. I was immediately reminded of what I already knew. People are people, no matter where, what color, rich or poor. We are all having a human experience. I read the description in the book out loud for further testimony. "The fool has grown up into a woman of the world. Leading a spiral dance, she is followed by her circle of friends and family. She skips through a chain of peyote buttons and flowers. These sacred plants part to let her by. She's come a long way. It no longer matters to her how she looks or that her clothes are torn. She takes her place among the children of the Earth… She may feel expanded and omnipotent because a major cycle in her life is completed and a new doorway opens."

All of this spoke to me, especially, "She takes her place among the children of the Earth," which landed directly in my heart. I was able to see and name the fear I had unjustifiably taken on. Fear for my safety and fear for another culture, a different nationality or mindset of people. For me, the *World* card was a message that I would be loved and protected anywhere I went in the world and that those differences are to be explored and celebrated, not feared. This was all the evidence we needed to stay the course and to continue on this great adventure.

Right after we became grounded in this decision, all of our, "Vamos a México pronto," chatter throughout the trailer park paid off. Jimmy came home elated saying one of our neighbors, Xavier was driving to Nogales, Mexico in just a few weeks to visit his family, and he had volunteered to take us there and put us on a Pacific bound train. We were buzzing with nervous excitement as it seemed this was really going to happen. I gave Quizno's my notice where no one shared my enthusiasm. They were all ho-hum grumpy because I only lasted two months and now they would have to hire and train someone else.

As light as we felt, there was a heaviness hanging over our final visitation with Robert. We knew how much he appreciated our visits, and us having been there. Jimmy felt especially bad not knowing when he would see him again. Ironically, Robert was more concerned about our safety than we were about his in jail, so we tried to reassure him by describing our loose vision. We told him we (I) had managed to save $1,600, and we'd continue to travel however long that lasts. We both had been creating jewelry and handicrafts to help fund our trip, and we figured if and when we did start to run out of money, it would be a cheap bus ticket to journey the long way back. He told us to be safe multiple times, and the brothers exchanged a long hug. I could truly feel his gratitude for us having been there the last few months.

We consolidated our belongings from the trailer back into our backpacks and were in Xavier's truck, headed for Nogales, laughing and trying out our basic Spanish. Before we knew it, we were in Mexico; riding on a rickety Third World train with an open hole in the floor for a bathroom and the orange glow of fireflies whizzing by outside. At one point, someone threw a rock through a window in the middle of the night, which sent shattering glass to the center of the train. It was loud, and it was poor, and it was hot, and it was dirty. And I realized that was exactly what was appealing to me because I was loving every minute of it!

Chapter 13

Flow

W e were officially in the international flow traveling with our hearts wide open. There was no Internet, and we had no guide book. We relied on the recommendations of the people we met along the way and the logistics of public transportation. I had turned heads before traveling on my own with my exotic-good-vibe-hitch-hiking-switchblade thing I had going, but together Jimmy and I were blowing minds. We were beyond happy to be on the road, or as Jimmy liked to call it, "High on The One." We were glowing with our rockstar-bearded-dreadlock-big-sunglasses-gypsy-circus energy. Jimmy, who was carrying his guitar, would stop and play a few crazy chords when people, especially kids, would stare at us. Usually it would be from the most far out song he could think of like Parliament's, "Everybody's got a little light under the sun, under the sun, under the sun…,"[15] which called even more attention to ourselves. We were exuding so much energy I don't think there was a

---

[15] Parliament "Flash Light", Track #6 on Funkentelechy vs. the Placebo Syndrome, Casablanca, 1977, vinyl

single person we came into contact with that was not curious about what we were on or what we were up to.

We usually had beachfront property where we pitched our tent, and swimming in the ocean equaled bathing. Local restaurant owners would let us use their restroom as we practiced our Spanish with them, bought bottled water, and occasionally ordered chips and guac. Our days were filled with smoking *mota*, making jewelry, studying Spanish and playing music. We practiced our massage techniques on each other with lavender olive oil that I made, which added an interesting savory smell to our already pungent natural aroma. In the evenings, we would play our short repertoire of Bob Marley songs and "La Bamba" with our handicrafts laid out on display. We'd sell our jewelry nearly exclusively to tourists and would always make new local friends. Depending on the size of the town and the tourist population, we were able to subsidize a lot of our trip with jewelry sales. We always felt welcome here and never felt threatened. This was confirmation that God does exist everywhere (go figure!) and that we *could* make a living with our own two hands.

This reality however, was not void of highs and lows. We experienced the high of meeting some gorgeous water sports guys who invited us to parasail in the tourist town of Ixtapa for free. Even though we refused their offer, explaining that flashy beach resorts weren't our kind of thing, they insisted. One minute we were sleeping on the beach in Zihuantanejo, and the next, we were not only partaking in an expensive tour in this fancy area, but we were also seeing it from above, soaring over the sparkling turquoise water in a parachute. Jimmy began to get jealous (low), especially if he was drinking. His imagination would run away with him thinking I wanted the water sports dudes or our new *cerveza amigos*. Those nights he would keep me awake angrily accusing me of wanting these men which I would first deny, then try reasoning with him, and finally I'd become angry too out of sheer exhaustion from not sleeping.

Miguel our *hashish amigo* prompted the worst of these fights while ironically, we were camped on a cliff overlooking Lover's Cove in Playa Zipolite. We had been in Mexico nearly two months, and I had stayed with our things while Jimmy went to the store. One of the only downsides of camping was that in most places we didn't trust leaving our "valuables" alone in the tent, which hey, we did have musical instruments, our jewelry and a film camera. He returned with a half drunken six pack and promises of a mescaline delivery, which we were excited about, having never done peyote. Sadly, when his new friend Miguel arrived, it was with hashish instead, which worked too, it just wasn't the new experience we were hoping for. We shared one gratitude bowl with him, and if he was making eyes at me, I didn't notice. But once he was gone Jimmy couldn't let it go. He **saw** and he **knew** how he was looking at me, which as I pointed out, even if he was, I wasn't to blame. Not willing to travel down an all-night jealousy road over this new ridiculousness, I told him we should just go our separate ways. I was done. I preferred to travel on my own than deal with his regular drama. I meant this, but even though we had been having an amazing experience without any problems thus far, part of me *was* scared to continue or at least to *camp* all alone. My intuition was telling me that I would be putting myself at too much risk by camping out in the open, as we had been, on my own. I was twenty years old. I saw other women, older women, living here on their own and young couples traveling together, but I hadn't seen any young females traveling alone. We were deep into Mexico, in the state of Oaxaca, getting close to the border of Guatemala where I really wanted to go, but could I, or should I do it sola? Jimmy broke my thought as he dramatically hurled his guitar on the rocks down below, doubled over in pain. He begged me not to leave him and promised it would never happen again. I was skeptical, but after a few rounds of apologies, tears and my hesitation, it seemed the safest thing to do. I prayed for the best while I cooked dinner in an uncomfortable silence. Jimmy repaired his guitar, and we began repairing our relationship.

I turned twenty-one in San Pedro La Laguna, Guatemala on mushroom honey. After having spent two months in Mexico, we scored a ride and crossed the border with an older European couple and their six-year-old son in a VW bus. We had an eventful week there, but as I was coming down from my mellow mushroom buzz, I found myself thinking about the fact that we had spent nearly all of our cash and probably should have ventured to the other side of Lake Atitlan towards an ATM sooner. We had wanted to stay in this beautiful place with the friends we had made through my birthday, but that decision left us with only enough money for the ferry the following morning.

We had been enchanted by this area and its people who were living very closely to the land. On the southern edge of the lake, stood three classic looking volcanoes. To the north, terraced gardens were etched along the steep slopes of the Sierra Madre mountain range. The Mayan descendants who populated the small villages surrounding the lake all wore colorful traditional clothing. Families could be seen bathing, and women washed clothes as children playfully swam in the lake. Enticed by all this natural beauty, we decided to dip in too, to fully absorb this area and the energy of the caldera. What we hadn't realized is that these daily activities; the washing of the clothes, the farming, and the simple little houses dotting the hillsides were contaminating the lake. One slight sip was all it took to send me from our tent to the bathroom and back for two days. Of course, they were communal bathrooms and at one point during one of my many trips there was a Spanish speaking young man in a stall nearby. I was so embarrassed at my lack of control, but all I could manage to communicate with my basic language skills was, "Caca de fuego," which I yelled over the door. For me, this translated as "shitting fire," but it literally means "fire poo." Oh well, as it was so perfectly in context, I am sure he understood.

One day while sitting at the hostel's communal picnic table, Jimmy and I were discussing how cool it would be to return to the U.S. with some Guatemalan fabric to sell and to share the colors and culture of this part of the world. "Or," Jimmy suggested, "Why don't we learn to make it ourselves?" I brushed this off, not knowing where to start and how difficult it would be to make yards of this material, but when a fabric angel came to visit us later that very day (literally, the woman's name was Angela) it seemed it was meant to be. Because our funds were tight, we settled on a very reasonable price for a weaving class for just me, and the next day I found myself in the local fabric shop choosing the colors of string I would use to make a small swatch of cloth. This was truly my first local moment of our trip. I stood next to Angela at the counter in the crowded shop and we held up the colors together, comparing and conversing with the other women in the store. I finally felt as if I was more than just a tourist and was actually part of the buzz of everyday life. For three days I sat at the loom in Angela's open air living room passing the baton *derecha y izquierda* just soaking up the comings and goings of her young daughter, neighbors, and chickens along with the view of the terraced gardens directly across from us and the lake that sat down below. The repetitiveness of the language she used made it easy for me to learn the new Spanish terms, but undoubtedly every time Angela would step out for a while, she would return to my hundreds of threads being tangled. I did manage to make a beautiful scarf/headpiece/tiny table runner which I still have, but I knew that teaching this to Jimmy and replicating it on our own would not be an option. The time I spent in Angela's home was invaluable, but we would have to save a small portion of money if we wanted to invest in fabric, or bags and pouches to sell upon our return, whenever that would be.

After experiencing the Sunday market in San Pedro, we crossed the lake and landed in Panajachel by late afternoon where we immediately began to look for a bank. Up until this point we had been slowly withdrawing from our U.S. checking account in Mexico with an ATM card that had the Plus/Pulse symbol. The first machine we found in Guatemala would not accept our card, even though there was a Plus symbol on the machine. Nor did the second. At the third we were becoming desperate, and getting the heavily armed guard's attention, we pointed to the symbol on our card, and then the machine. He replied with a grunt and a pivot, pointing the butt of his gun at the MasterCard sticker in the window. We realized nearly everyone else in the world probably did have a credit card and that obviously, the banking system had changed dramatically when we crossed the border.

We would have to try our luck at selling our wares. We followed fingers pointing us towards *artesania,* which eventually led to long rows of steep vending competition. Most people were packing up though, as we set our black cloth on the ground. We exchanged greetings with the neighbor to the left of us. His name was Teo. A nice long-haired, classic looking Andean Chilean some ten years older than us. As we set our things out, I made an extra special effort to address the few tourists still left in the market. The sun was beginning to get low and if we couldn't sell anything it would mean a night on the street of this small city which we hadn't had to do thus far in our travels. As I turned on my charm to the thinning public, Jimmy and Teo sat conversing with one another. He was an artist and a musician so the two of them talked about music and the bamboo flutes that Jimmy was now making. Teo had been staying up in the mountains north of Guatemala City on a volunteer farm. I shot Jimmy a dirty look for squandering precious time making small talk. He needed to help me sell something. We *had* to sell something. This prompted him to share our quandary.

Teo had cash problems of his own. He was broke and waiting for his English girlfriend's new Visa card to arrive in the mail. I began to grow even more impatient (with both of them now) as Teo rattled on about the volunteer farm where he had taken refuge, all in Español. He had been there a month... the owner was a wealthy Englishman... he was lonely and he enjoyed having foreigners come stay... blah blah blah… guest houses... gardens... a sauna... even drinks, marijuana and cocaine if they are so inclined. "Okay, that does sound like an excellent place to be broke, I interjected, "pero no tenemos *nada* de *dinero* (but we don't have *any money*)" in a tone that let them both know I was now officially stressed out.

Teo told us not to worry. The owner had given him $200 to come down the mountain to check the post office for his girlfriend's credit card, print and pass out fliers for the farm and to try to get more volunteers. He was confident that he still had enough money for a hotel that night and to get all of us back to the farm. If not, Ebenezer (the owner) would pay cab fare when we arrived. *Wait, what!? This broke South American street vendor that we just* **happened** *to set our things next to had been sent on a mission to bring more volunteers back to a volunteer farm? He was going to pay our hotel room* **and** *get us all back to this farm? We were saved!???* After praising Jah, I was immediately confronted with my shortsightedness that had nearly interrupted the natural flow of events that was unfolding between Jimmy and Teo. I realized I could have easily repelled Teo with my intensity, being so stressed out. And by being so fixated on one solution, I had nearly overlooked our salvation that was coming in another form. I wondered how often this happens; that we allow our emotions to spill over and are unable to see what is right in our cup.

The guys continued their friendly exchange, completely oblivious to my mood or epiphany. Teo also knew of a magic ATM machine in Guatemala City that worked for lots of foreigners. He suggested we try that on our way to the farm, and if it worked, maybe not go to the farm at all. We were officially nestling in under Teo's wings. We gave vending another half hour or so as he poured over all the details of the next day's adventure and our final destination. As night set in, we went to perform music in a restaurant with a few of Teo's friends. Their brass section completely blew our usual renditions out of the water. We were cut out of the little tips they earned, but still given a few slices of pizza. I thoroughly enjoyed being part of this improvised band. We all left together, wandering through the alleyways and dark streets of Panajachel. The trumpet player occasionally sent a few sexy notes out into the night, and we all shared a bottle of whiskey and a joint. Despite all we had been through that day, I felt extremely grateful to be part of this group. I also felt special and protected being the only girl. We circled to pass a joint one more time and after a few more snips out of a bottle we said our goodbyes. As promised, Teo treated us to a double bed in a shared hotel room with him. No strings attached.

In the morning he shared a simple meal of bread and tomatoes with us, as well as the fact that his farm money was starting to run very thin. He thought he had enough to make it all the way back, but we still had to stop in Antigua for him to check the post office one last time. We tried our luck at vending and other ATMs there, but *nada* and still no credit card. Teo's stories of the farm began to sound more and more unbelievable. There were horses, a small schoolhouse, gardens and a private sauna for the volunteers that Teo had been restoring. The owner bought them weed and cocaine and though he refused to snort it, he indulged as well, pouring coke into his drink at night. All this in a setting that overlooked a beautiful valley and two volcanoes sounded too good to be true, but what could we do? At this point we were along for the full ride.

After one final and fruitless attempt at the Antigua post office the next morning, we all set off for Guatemala City which is subdivided into numbered zones. As the bus entered the city, we passed from zone to zone. It looked just as dangerous as people had made it out to be. We had to disembark at Zone 8 and take another bus to Zone 1. Once there, Teo seemed to know the way. He led us through a huge park where there was an event going on. We passed by informative booths making our way to the next block where the magic ATM resided. We waited in line for this machine that had worked for so many others, but unfortunately not for us. This is when Teo had to tell us there was no money left. Not even enough to take the other bus we needed to leave the city and then a taxi for the remainder of the way up to the farm. The sun was getting low, and this time we ran the risk of being absolutely destitute on the streets of the much worse, much more dangerous Guatemala City. Zone 1 did not look like the kind of neighborhood we'd want to be homeless in.

Teo offered a possible solution. We walked a few blocks to a popular hostel for Peace Corps volunteers. Along the way he confirmed that the last bus for the day, the bus that we *needed* to be on, would pass by at 6:30 p.m. Teo explained the current plan once more as we arrived at the wrought iron gate, and he rang the buzzer to the hostel. He was sending me in alone, basically pimping me out. Not my body, but our jewelry, to make just enough money for bus fare. The weight of our welfare now all rested upon me. I anxiously listened as he repeated we would need U.S. *six dollars* to get ourselves out of the city to the main village near the farm. He told me to sell anything I needed to, even my most expensive jewelry, just to get the six dollars. I nodded somberly that I understood, and he added the final detail of the plan, that from the village, we would have to take a taxi the rest of the way up the mountain and have the owner pay the fare upon arrival.

Assuming I was a guest as well, a woman opened the gate and continued shuffling along the Spanish tile leaving me in her wake. The guys reminded me that we only had fifteen minutes before the last bus would pass, as the gate clicked closed and locked behind me. I walked into the central garden where there were a few tables in a common area and luckily someone, a man (helpful), was sitting and writing. "Hello," I nervously said as I sat right down alongside him. I didn't have time to be charming. I just needed to express the magnitude of the situation. I explained, matter-of-factly without an air of complaint, that we had no access to our money, not one Guatemalan quetzal, or a place to stay. I got right to the point, stating that if we didn't have bus fare to get out of the city there was a chance we would be homeless on the streets of Guatemala City. I began to unwrap the black cloth that held all of our jewelry. I expressed that I wasn't begging for money and offered him anything, anything at all for the bus fare. "Just thirty quetzales or six U.S. dollars." I showed him my expensive intricately beaded necklaces. He began to touch a simple bracelet and spoke with an English accent for the first time. "So, what you're telling me is if I don't buy something from you for at least six dollars right NOW, you and your friends will be on the streets tonight and that's supposed to be MY FAULT?"

"Yes, we may be on the streets tonight," I spoke quickly, "but that's not your fault. Obviously, this is *our* problem, and I am sorry to bring you into it, but it is *only* six dollars, and you will have something to show for it. That bracelet is only worth four. Take ANYTHING, really ANYTHING for six dollars." I held up necklace after necklace, rattling off the normal prices. "This is normally thirty dollars, this thirty-five, forty…"

More than five minutes must have already passed. My legs began to bop up and down feeling the time crunch. Our solution unzipped his Guatemalan change purse and counted various quetzal notes. He was short! He begrudgingly stood up and went back to his room to look for more. I let out a big sigh realizing I had been holding my breath. I could only hope he would actually come back and not just close himself up in his room ignoring our situation. I got to work on putting everything away and getting ready to run to the bus stop. I left out his bracelet of choice and one other which was similar as a token of my appreciation. Thankfully, he returned and bitterly handed me the money. He refused the other bracelet saying he hadn't wanted the first one to begin with. I thanked him profusely and ran out the door. The boys were nowhere to be found so I began running to where the bus would be passing. It was there! Teo was standing with one foot on the street and one on the stairs of the bus, with his hand on the metal handrail as if he was holding it in place for me. I raced up the stairs and Teo followed. The doors closed behind us, and we walked towards the center where Jimmy was sitting. I nodded to them both as I sat down, and relief spread across their faces. "That was horrible," I told them, referring to my stressful interaction with the English man, as I put my head down on the seat in front of me. I coughed up my earnings to Pimp Teo and he paid the man who walked the aisle charging each passenger. As I looked out the window, the sun was setting, and the streets were becoming quiet. I was thankful for not having to endure a night in what is probably one of the most dangerous cities I had ever been to.

Teo grabbed tobacco, rolling papers, peanut butter and a few other nonessential items from the little village store where they normally shopped and told them to put it on the farm owner, Ebenezer's tab. Our old wooden paneled station wagon of a taxi complained and sputtered all the way up the steep dirt road the remainder of the way towards the farm. The driver began to tell us he knows exactly where he's going. One of his daughters worked there once helping with Ebenezer's children. One of his, "Thirty-eight sons and daughters," he told us laughing proudly. After all I had been through that day, I was ready to strangle anyone for having thirty-eight children, much less bragging about it. The guy was hideous with missing teeth, but as he pointed out, tall and with green eyes, so the women loved him. *Ick! What a chauvinist! How much longer? Are we there yet? I have to go to the bathroom!*

The last stretch became two cement strips leading the rest of the way up. We passed what Teo told us was Ebenezer's private church which curiously enough was built out of bundles of sticks. We wound around the top of the valley now and soon Ebenezer's giant hacienda came into view. As we pulled up, Ebenezer himself came out and before we had a chance to introduce ourselves, a heated discussion ensued between him, Teo and occasionally the taxi driver. Words like "credit card" and "money" flew around as did Ebenezer's hands. He did not seem happy, so to avoid confrontation we slowly crept away from the taxi and toward the entrance of his home. We had just enough time to take in his arched entryway. It was like a mansion straight out of an old school movie. Both of the walls in the entrance were lined with historical looking portraits in large gaudy gold frames containing who I assumed were Ebenezer's ancestors. There were men in full English riding gear, holding switches and rifles looking to be on a fox hunt and a woman in a Victorian gown seated on a throne-like chair with her hair perfectly spiraling down from either side of a bun. In between each painting was a saddle stand with either a beautiful English or western riding saddle with its matching bridle hanging below. In the center of all of this was a mounted zebra head, the cherry on top.

As we were taking all of this in, we were finally welcomed in the most eccentric manner. "Helllooooooooo, I am Eh-be-neeeee-zer. What do you think of my howwwwsssss?" We turned to see Ebenezer, a well-dressed classically rich looking man with a light complexion and white hair standing with his arms wide open as if to say, *It's mine, all mine, welcome.* I should have been thanking him profusely, but my blood sugar was extremely low. He seemed to embody every obnoxious rich stereotype, so instead the words, "Well I don't know, we just got here and it's dark," came tumbling out of my mouth. I felt horrible right after I said it, but as it turned out, my initial assessment wasn't too far off.

Chapter 14

Volunteer Mansion

Everything about the farm proved to be true. Ebenezer was a lonely aristocrat (about fifty years old) looking to socialize with international volunteers, specifically of the female variety. In fact, he told us to come join him for a drink in his study that first night after dinner. I'm not sure if it was his social stature or the fear of being overheard, but he referred to marijuana as "da English" whispering, and "da co-cah-eee-na" as "da Spanish." He had "da Spanish" but was waiting for more "English" to arrive. His friend who was the Guatemalan equivalent of a DEA (U.S. government Drug Enforcement Administration) agent would be delivering more confiscated weed to the farm. Ebenezer made a point of telling us he didn't snort the Spanish, he just put it in his drink. Once the English arrived, we could have a personal stash to take back to our guesthouse which would be added to our tab. We were also told we could request any personal items from the store by adding them to the weekly grocery list to be paid back at a later date once we had our funds again.

About our funds. Ebenezer was beyond narcissistic. That first night he took the time to explain his wealth and his ancestry, mostly addressing me when he spoke. His forefathers were English and some of the first major landowners to settle in what is now Los Angeles, California. He had old photographs of property on the walls of his study to back up his story. When he finally did ask us something about ourselves, I was able to inquire about an international phone call and the best place to wire money, assuming that if either set of parents could help us out we would pay them back later. I expressed that if he gave us his phone number, our parents could call us right back. He waved his hand in the air dismissing me with, "Yes yes, tomorrow," wanting to know more personal information regarding our pedigree. This translated to "mañana," which was not a good sign because as they say in Latin America, "tomorrow never comes." But having just arrived, I didn't want to be more of a nuisance than we already were, so I engaged in superficial conversation, not pressing the matter.

We spent the next few days familiarizing ourselves with our new housemates (Teo and his girlfriend Nyra), the other volunteers (three more Americans), and the inner workings of the farm. Nyra was a curious looking young English girl with creamy brown skin and thick coke bottle glasses. She and Teo both spent their time working on jewelry, though they were more inspired when "the English" was there at the farm. They were trying to build their inventory so when they finally did leave the farm, they would have more to sell. We had a lot in common with them both. They were in need of new materials and tired of some of their old, so we set about trading clasps, stones and ideas, talking and creating together well into the evenings.

For my first chore on the farm, I was separated from Jimmy and instructed to weed Ebenezer's flower beds. I was working right along the windows of the house where he could watch me, which was completely uncomfortable. After just a half a day of that I moved myself along, helping the others and gaining another perspective. All three of the other volunteers had found The Finca San Isidro on this thing called the Internet. It had been advertised as a reforestation project with over six thousand trees to plant in the valley. To their dismay, they had actually discovered that Ebenezer was in fact part of the deforestation problem and continued to be. They suspected he was logging illegally, with men and oxen removing huge trees from the other side of his property. He had purchased about 200 small pine trees to be planted in an area that first needed to be cleared of garbage. To prepare the soil to plant these trees, their job was to remove the trash where a local family had been living as caretakers for over twenty years, just throwing their garbage on the ground. So now, these three were spending their vacation not on a reforestation project as they had planned, but cleaning up this steep hillside on a rich man's private property. They were only beginning to work through the first layer of this family's household garbage; removing plastic bags, old clothing, shoes, rope, etc. when I arrived on the scene. This was their first grievance. Their second was Teo and Nyra. Who, according to them, "Always slept in and never helped."

When we were finally able to use Ebenezer's phone to call home, Jimmy tried his dad first. Since my parents had completely disapproved of this trip, we were reluctant to ask them for help. Jimmy's dad had a lot of financial responsibilities, many of which weren't really his own. His dad and stepmom's home had a revolving door, which openly accepted struggling family members. They were constantly helping to raise rebellious or displaced cousins, nieces, nephews and grandchildren whose parents were also struggling. Jimmy pleaded with him and told his father he could repay him with his Alaskan Dividend Fund (the annual oil money shares the state pays to each of its residents). Apparently, this was something Jimmy did every year. He would ask his dad for a loan, knowing his dividend money would be coming in October, which at that time was in the neighborhood of two thousand dollars each resident. Every year his dad said it was the last time he would help him like that. Even though his dad was a big softie, he insisted he was strapped and that we should try my parents instead.

My parents listened intently but seemed hesitant to send us money straight away. Alternatively, they quickly offered another solution. My sister would be graduating from high school, and they had been asking if I was planning on coming to Miami for her graduation. Their repeatedly *asking* me felt more like *pressure*. They had offered to buy me a plane ticket, but I had kept putting them off, telling them I didn't know where I'd be. Now, seeing as though I probably wasn't going *anywhere* with no access to our money, they suggested I fly out of Guatemala City. I could spend one week with my family and withdraw our own funds from the bank myself. I was a bit shocked by their response. I did want to attend Amy's graduation, and being in the U.S. just for a week or so would be interesting, but it was over a month away. That would mean remaining on the farm dead broke and at Ebenezer's mercy for much longer than we had anticipated. The only explanation I could think of for them not wiring me any money, was that they didn't trust me to pay it back. And, I thought, *now they have me right where they want me,* **grounded**, *so we can all be together for my sister's graduation.* Sensing there wouldn't be much room for renegotiating our lifeline, I didn't know what other option we had. With the pressure of having made an international call from Ebenezer's home phone, I agreed. Once the ticket was purchased, my parents called the farm to give me the details.

When the English arrived, time began to pass more quickly. Ebenezer's married friend brought his lover up to the farm along with a kilo of tightly wrapped shwag weed and more of the Spanish. Apparently, there was so much hype around this big drug bust they had made, he had to wait until things simmered down and was able to take a brick without anyone noticing. Now those of us who lived in the "lazy household" were all happily beading, playing music and singing into the evening.

I enjoyed spending time with Fabia, a beautiful, older, Guatemalan woman who had raised Ebenezer on the farm. She wore her hair in two long braids and kept baby chicks warm in the pockets of her apron. I would practice my Spanish while helping Fabia and chatting with her and her niece Esmeralda who also lived on the farm. Ebenezer treated them like servants, which only solidified my disapproval of the extremely wealthy. They both worked long hours as cooks and caretakers but were never welcomed to sit and eat with us. They slept atop cardboard on exposed box springs in the west wing of Ebenezer's mansion. One day Fabia asked me to go to the pantry for some canned goods. Esmeralda followed me in and pressed me against the wall. "What are these?" she asked, squeezing my breasts and laughing wildly. I placed my hands firmly on top of hers and held her away. She interlocked her fingers with mine and we were palm to palm, pressing into one another, engaged in a "hand war" of sorts. I remained strong and calm. In broken Spanish, I told her they were breasts or *tetas* the only word I knew in Spanish and that she had them too. I wriggled away from her and ran back to Fabia without the canned goods to tattle that Esmeralda was touching my *tetas*.

Fabia began to yell at Esmeralda, none of which I understood, eventually getting the cans she requested on her own. Neither one of the women ever joined us for meals, but I would be sure to keep my distance from Esmeralda from now on. After lunch, she entered the kitchen to help Fabia clean up. I told Jimmy what had happened, and we excused ourselves promptly from the table. As we left the kitchen, out of the corner of my eye, I saw Esmeralda pulling something out of a drawer. Then, she came running after us. It was a large syringe with a needle in it, the type used for injecting meat with flavor. Jimmy was out the front door first yelling for me to close the door behind me, but it had stained glass panels, some of which were missing. Like a psycho in a horror movie, Esmeralda swung the syringe around out of the broken window with one hand and fought to open the door with the other. I held the door closed with both hands and was able to stand back as she jabbed the long needle aimlessly through the air laughing like a crazy person. I knew she wouldn't be able to open the door, but we couldn't stay like this all day. Jimmy tried to communicate, urging her to be *tranquila* that we were her *amigos,* and she paused. But then, she began viscously swinging the needle in the air again. We decided we would give her a few minutes to see if she tired, and if not, we would make a run for it down the hill to our house. We doubted she could catch us or do much damage if she did. We were two against one.

Imagining that this young girl probably had nothing better to do all day than wait at that door, we decided to make a mad dash down the hill. It was her traditional wrap skirt that restricted her stride to less than half of ours. A third of the way down the hill she gave up as we rounded the corner to our house. We arrived breathless, relaying the magnitude of the situation to Teo and Nyra. They were emotionless as they explained that Esmeralda was severely troubled and very immature for her age. She could barely speak Spanish, much less read or write. She had thrown herself at Teo during one of their guitar lessons. They suggested we just keep our distance and not mention it to Ebenezer. Teo said he would talk to her. He thought to impress upon her that if it happened again, she would probably get kicked off the farm. Great. It wasn't our intention to contribute to her downward spiral in life. I *knew* a month was longer than we needed to be here and was looking forward to my sister's graduation more and more every day.

Miami day eventually came, and Ebenezer drove me (along with his children who had been visiting for the weekend) into Guatemala City. He dropped them off at their private school and then took me to the airport. I had a whirlwind visit with both my immediate and extended family that were in Miami to celebrate my sister's high school graduation. My mom loaded me down with lots of health food items as well as paper, activity books and crayons for the little schoolhouse situated on the farm, which in this case, I was actually happy to receive. I had told her the school was in need of supplies, knowing it was something we would both love to help with. I had everything packed in a box in addition to my backpack. When I got to the ticket counter at the airport, I was informed that just yesterday a ban was placed on all boxes going to Guatemala. The only solution they offered me was to have the contents of the box wrapped in plastic like a giant everlasting gobstopper. The plastic wrap people were nice enough to add a bit of rope like a handle in the wrapping, but it was incredibly heavy and hard to handle. I had to return to the ticket counter to check my awkward plastic ball and then hurry if I was going to make my flight. I think it is a universal law that whenever we are in a hurry, things start to go wrong, *or* we begin to hyper-focus on obstacles that under normal circumstances, we would hardly notice. The security line was one of these obstacles. It was the old kind of security line, when we just needed to pass through a metal detector to board our individual flights. But this was a long line that was servicing a number of flights, when I *really* needed to board mine. It was moving so slowly, that I began studying the back of everyone's heads doing a little nervous dance in place. I noticed one head in particular, just a few people ahead of me. It was a beautiful head with long blonde hair and one single dread that still held the remnants of an old hair wrap. I scanned her body. Cute new Birkenstocks, a beautiful rayon hippie-type jumper. If I hadn't known better, I would think it was Lily, Holding's ex-girlfriend from Chico. I called her name out loud and low and behold, the head turned around in line. "Òhhhhh My God! Michelle, sweethearttt, how are you?" She was headed to Jamaica. I told her I was meeting my boyfriend back in Guatemala, but that we would love to come to Jamaica for Reggae Sunsplash, something Jimmy and I *had* talked about. She quickly gave me the name and number of her boyfriend who had a house where she would be staying during the festival, inviting us to stay with them. Our conversation was cut short as she made it through the checkpoint, and we both had to run off in different directions. I was blown away that not only had I seen someone I knew from California on the complete opposite side of the country, but I had just run into the one person, *the only person*, that I felt slightly insecure or jealous about. And of course, she was as friendly and bubbly as she always was with me.

After the plane took off, I was able to sit in the enormity of this encounter. For one, if I had been able to check my box, we probably never would have ran into each other. I asked myself why was I even studying people's heads in line, or the better question, what prompted me to actually say her name and think that I'd get a response? My mind was racing now! *Why would I see Lily of all people, the person I had been jealous of? Was I supposed to ask her about Holding? Damn! I should have asked her about Holding, but there was no time!* As I searched for deeper meaning, the pilot announced Cuba was to our left, and looking out of the window, I saw my answer. There was a perfect double rainbow over the Caribbean Sea! It almost made me cry. We were family, and we were both rainbows, unique with our own vibrant colors and personalities. There was no need to compare myself to anyone, ever. I wondered if she was seeing these same rainbows on her way to Jamaica.

Jimmy had agreed to meet me at the airport in Guatemala City as I was nervous about the complicated public transportation through the zones by myself, and I had a lot to carry. After looking for Jimmy for what felt like an hour in the airport, I had him paged in Spanish which sounded something like, "Atención! Señor Jimmmiii blahblahblahblah ...," If he were in the airport, he would never realize his name was being called on the loudspeaker. After another attempt to clarify the announcement, I gave up, knowing he was most likely there looking for me as he said he would be, but I had no idea where. I headed out toward the street with plans to mill around there for a while, but the insistent taxi drivers wore on me quickly. To avoid them, I decided to walk toward the bus stop. A fourteen-year-old boy I met and his little brother quickly swept me onto the bus helping me with my heavy backpack and my awkward oversized plastic wrapped ball. The boys rode with me the entire length of the first bus ride and then waited for the next bus with me. When they explained they would be taking that same bus back to the airport, I understood they solely rode that bus to help me, and I would need to pay them enough to cover their bus fares and something for their effort. Now with my temporary guardians gone, I couldn't help feeling frustrated. Not only did I have all this weight to lug around by myself, but I was also beginning to realize that traveling with a small Ziplock bag of good weed in my most feminine oral cavity was a rookie maneuver. Why on earth did I use a Ziplock bag? After spending the entire time worrying about my things strapped down and tarped on top of the bus in the rain, and then the taxi ride, that this time I paid, I finally arrived back at the volunteer farm and went straight to our guest house. This was like waking to a dream and discovering it was in fact, real. The farm did really exist and was navigable. Teo and Nrya were there, but not Jimmy. It was as I suspected. He had gone to the airport to look for me. He had no money, but had left with another girl, a new arrival at the farm who I hadn't met yet. Upon his eventual arrival, he was elated to see I had made it back. He introduced me to his most recent travel partner, a cute young hippie girl whom I had to pay back for his unnecessary expenses that day. I felt a twinge of resentment and jealousy. Oh how quickly we forget life's rainbow lessons!

I had recovered our last $600, half of which we wanted to invest in Guatemalan textiles for resale. We began to make plans to leave the farm. Ebenezer was growing increasingly more impatient with Teo and Nyra threatening to kick them out. They saw us (and our funds) as a safety net and began to make plans to leave together. I did not want to pay their travel expenses, but Teo had rescued us, so we agreed to help get them to Antigua to check the post for Nyra's credit card.

The bus from Guatemala City to this beautiful tourist town started out very crowded. It was a Canadian school bus and people were sitting three to a seat and still having to stand in the aisle. We stayed on until the end of the route at the terminal when it began to clear out. It was very odd when an older man sat next to Jimmy and I, when there was clearly no need to sit three to a seat anymore. I sensed something strange so from the window seat I said, "shady character," to Jimmy, but continued to look out the window taking in all the colors and culture of our new environment as did Jimmy. The older gentleman got off the bus just before us. As we got up and began walking toward the door of the bus, Jimmy's belongings began to fall out of his carry-on Mexican bag. We both launched into panic mode noticing his bag had been slit open. Jimmy frantically searched for his wallet and passport. The wallet which contained slightly more than $300, the last of our money that we had split, was nowhere to be found. Thankfully though his passport was not stolen as well. This was a major setback. We now had ourselves, Teo, Nyra, and Caldus their traveling teenage cat on a string, to house and feed with our last three hundred dollars.

Chapter 15

Big Monopoly

We sat with Teo and Nyra for a few days vending on the streets of Antigua trying to recuperate some of the money which was stolen without much luck. Antigua is a tourist and local handicraft mecca, making it a buyers' market. I spent more time people watching than actually speaking with potential customers. I marveled at the resilience of the people around me. There was a woman without any legs balancing a large bundle on her head while she used her hands on the dirty pavement like crutches. I thought of how at home in the U.S. this woman would probably qualify for government assistance and in the very least have a wheelchair, maybe even a driver or a special car that she could drive herself. It occurred to me how sterile and "behind closed doors" everything is in America. Most people drive everywhere and when they get home, they shut their garage door to enjoy their privacy and the comforts they work so hard to afford. Here people took to the streets walking. Life was more difficult, but colorful and out in the open for everyone to see. I absorbed the chatter all around me.

Friends and neighbors laughed and greeted one another in no visible rush to get anywhere, truly in the here and now. Most likely *this* is what had drawn me to this particular part of the world. A place where maybe they had less material possessions, but they clearly had more time to enjoy life without the stress of a mortgage or a car payment. From what I could tell, chasing the American dream wasn't a thing here nor was depression. These people had the kind of self-generated *inner* peace and happiness I was looking to maintain in my life.

On the farm, the four of us had discussed traveling to the Caribbean Coast to the village of Livingston, Guatemala. Jimmy and I decided to set off in that direction to change our scenery and hopefully our luck as well. Teo and Nyra now had a running tab with us for their hotel and bus fare. We needed to cut our ties, or we would all four end up broke again. They managed to squeeze a little more travel assistance out of us, accompanying us on the bus as far as Puerto Barrios. It was difficult, but the following day we left them at the ferry terminal with no money wishing them luck and telling them we would see them in Livingston. To our dismay, as we sat and waited on the boat in the heat of the day, we saw Teo, Nyra, and of course Caldus boarding the ferry. They had traded some jewelry for their boat fare, and we set off together once again.

Upon arrival, a black dreadlock Rasta greeted Jimmy and I shouting, "Welcome to Africa Rastafari!" We saw this as a good omen and felt at home immediately. We found rooms which used to serve as a dentist office in what was formerly a gated business plaza for $3 a night. Jimmy and I paid for a week in advance, and Teo paid for one night, planning to pay as they went, assuming they could sell some jewelry. Livingston had a unique style of nightlife which we quickly became a part of. Foreigners from around the globe would meander after dark, walking by the various venders slowly to see if something might catch their eye. Later, the locals would come out playing and singing an Afro-Caribbean style rhythm called Punta. They would use drumsticks to beat turtle shells loudly and shake rattles made of coconuts and gourds. They traveled from bar to restaurant entertaining the tourists collecting spare change and making Livingston a special place.

Our first few days in Livingston we did well vending and making new friends. This was not a popular tourist destination, so we were some of the only artisan vendors. Teo and Nyra were also successful and we were relieved to see them start to pay their debt back. Being open and friendly with everyone, I became friends with another sweet little old Guatemalan woman, my second grandmother this trip. She would sell her homemade, warm coconut bread from a big basket in the afternoons. She'd come limping over to me, knowing I was a sure sale. She would sit on the curb holding my hand, trying to converse with me and inviting me to her house every day. Then, at sunset, like clockwork, a transwoman would come out in her high heels and sexy halter top, pushing her girlfriend's baby carriage down the road. The girlfriend would sidle up to me and practice her English exclaiming, "I love you," over and over again. Coconut grandma would laugh and roll her eyes, taking her cue to go, leaving me with this horny female admirer.

Jimmy and I would play hacky sack while we were vending to help pass the time. Back in the day, I was pretty good. I could pull off foot stalls, back stalls, and even my famous *chest* stall. As a young couple approached us, I told Jimmy that the guy looked like my friend Esteban that I had told him about. Esteban was a friend from high school a few years older than me, who had been living in Costa Rica, painting murals for some time. We had heard word via old-school telephone and mutual friends that there was a possibility we would both be traveling through Central America at the same time, but that's all we knew. Central America is a large region that consists of *seven* countries. Within those seven countries there is a plethora of tourist destinations; mountain towns, lakes, ruins, hot springs, coastal villages, cities, etc. But, sure enough, it *was* Esteban in Livingston, Guatemala, which is pretty far off the beaten path on the Gringo Trail. Just like seeing Lily, there was no way in my mind that this was a coincidence. It's not possible that our paths could cross without our energy somehow being aligned or drawing us towards one another. We couldn't believe it. Astonishment, love, hugs and excitement ensued. We were completely swept away in the moment of seeing one another, of how this could happen, exchanging news of old friends and forgetting all about our partners, uncomfortably standing by as onlookers. We quickly found our manners, introducing everyone, sensing tension and possible jealousy from both. We made plans to meet up later and talked about hiking to the waterfalls at Rio Dulce the following day.

We spent the next day swimming naked in the natural pools at the waterfall while exchanging information with Esteban and his German girlfriend Hanna. Esteban shared details about where he had been living in Dominical, Costa Rica and where they had been on their travels. We listened, but our compass seemed to be shifting away from Costa Rica and more towards Reggae Sunsplash in Jamaica. They were going to keep moving north the next day and as business had slowed, we thought we would move south into Honduras.

We had heard of a river crossing to Honduras which would save us time and money that only cost a few quetzals each in the narrowest of motorized dugout canoes. We headed to the Finca Inca by bus (two hours) where we were reminded to have our passports stamped at the office de migración. I have no idea where we actually were. Possibly the Motagua River crossing, but it was super primitive at that time. As we traveled slowly through chocolate colored water, spearfishermen would pop their heads up waving and smiling with their large goggles on. Our boat captain explained that the river actually divided the two countries. We were surrounded by dense jungle and when we finally arrived, the only structure there to receive us was a bamboo shack behind a simple home on the riverbank. This served as the currency exchange. With no one in sight, our fellow passengers hollered, announcing our arrival. A señora came waddling out, all chatty and smiling. We patiently waited as she clicked away on her shitty calculator, pausing and waving its mini solar panels in search of the sun. Once we exchanged our quetzals for lempira, we were on our way. Our new travel companions kindly waited for us to walk the trail together back to the highway where we could catch a bus. The Bay

Islands were all the buzz, so we set out for the city of San Pedro Sula and made our way south along the coast.

I fell in love with Utila, the most laid back of the three Bay Islands which attracts backpackers from all over the world. A very nice dive shop owner allowed us to camp in the yard of his guest house for free. We were able to snorkel right off of the nearby dirt airstrip. This became my happy place. I would snorkel through what seemed like trails in the tall sea grass, to brain coral gardens teaming with fish. I'd scare myself by swimming to the shelf edge where the bottom dropped to about 100 feet and it became a deep blue abyss. I'd imagine a shark coming into view from the vast blue and then panic, making my way back to the safety of the brain coral. I would snorkel there once or twice a day, sometimes with Jimmy, but mostly on my own.

Utila is rich with pirate history which was evident in the light skin tone and the local pirate dialect spoken here. During the day, we had a hunter/gatherer budget type experiment going where we were discovering that man could *not* live off of free coconuts and mangos alone. I was beginning to surrender to the fact that money (or some sort of currency) was essential, even in the tropics, where the fruit was falling from the trees. We ended up having to break down to buy some groceries and cheeseless quesadillas from the baleada food cart lady. At night, business was picking up, and we were selling more handicrafts than we had thus far. We were the only artisan vendors there in that moment and we set up in front of the popular discoteca, Bucket of Blood. Over the weekend we sold $60 worth of inventory each day. Jimmy had discovered how to make small coconut pipes using the *coquitos* and a small piece of bamboo for the stem. We were also making our own bamboo beads, using a tiny hand saw blade, sandpaper and burning each end. With no other competition, I was highly motivated to produce more inventory and had been nagging Jimmy to do the same. For days he had been blowing me off saying that his creative juices would start flowing again once we found some weed. Now that we had scored some smoke, I was insistent that he contribute to our financial wellbeing. "Ohhhhh kayyyyyy BIG MONOPOLY," he finally conceded, which as ridiculous as this was, it was the sheer irony of his name calling (the fact that I had intentionally made all of my life choices to *not* be part of the system) that hooked me. I became unraveled. "*Really*, you're calling *me Big Monopoly?* What a fucking insult! I'm living out of a tent and selling jewelry on *the street* in Central America, for God's sakes. THAT IS NOT BIG MONOPOLY!" I hardly came up for air. "WE ARE RUNNING OUT OF MONEY AND THERE IS A HUGE OPPORTUNITY FOR US TO GET AHEAD HERE. DON'T YOU WANT TO CONTINUE TRAVELING? DON'T YOU WANT TO GO TO JAMAICA OR AT LEAST HAVE ENOUGH MONEY TO PAY FOR A BUS TICKET BACK HOME?"

"OK, *relax*," was his only reply as he begrudgingly dug his tools out of the tent to get to work.

"Fucking take it back. Say I'm not Big Monopoly."

"You're not Big Monopoly. Just relax. I'm going to help make shit."

We sat in the yard of the guesthouse working, but I was still fuming and I could not relax. I was realizing (yet again) that I was clearly a much more motivated vagabond than him. I continued my lecture, stressing the fact that we currently did not have enough money to get ourselves back to the states. He was going to have to help me, and we were going to have to work together and *hustle*, if we wanted to continue our journey or get ourselves home. I knew Jimmy really didn't care. He embodied bliss, no matter what. He was happy just being together, and he probably *could* live off of mangoes and coconut alone. But I knew that we were going to need more.

Everyone who was staying at the guesthouse was doing a dive course or had paid for multiple dives which included their stay. There was a communal kitchen, but we cooked outside on our camp stove trying not to get in the way of Dave's (the shop owner) paying customers. We would exchange pleasantries with other guests, but annoyingly the most common question we received was, "If you aren't diving, what are you doing here?" So, even though what happened next made sense, we hardly saw it coming.

One of the girls from the guesthouse had her purse with all of its contents stolen (her passport, credit cards and all her money) in broad daylight while she was out diving. Dave came over and listened to her rant asking, "What are they doing here?" In her mind we were the number one suspects. Or, as she insisted while yelling as if we weren't actually there, "They had to have seen something. They just sit here all day smoking weed and doing nothing!"

Unfortunately, we hadn't seen anything, and of course, we would never do such a thing. We had an excellent alibi. We had gone out to buy tuna for the kittens we had promised a former guest we would continue to feed. Dave expressed that he believed and trusted us, but he had to ask us to leave. He was receiving too many negative reviews from his paying customers. Hindsight, we probably should have looked for another place to stay on the island because on the big monopoly business front things were going so well for us. But no regrets. I do believe that everything happens for a reason, and so for whatever reason, we shoved off for the more developed resort island of Roatan that we had been warned against.

We touched ground in Puerto Cortes, a bustling, dirty shipping port full of large container ships loaded with fruit and coffee going to the first world. We made our way to the main loading dock and inquired about a free ride to Roatan, Jamaica or possibly Miami. After speaking to a number of people coming and going, including our new Rasta friend, Lucas, we learned that the huge boats were mainly headed to New Orleans. Lucas suggested we try the fishing docks for a free ride to Roatan and told us we were welcome to stay with him in Travesia, a seldom traveled beach town a little ways down the coast. Ending our conversation, he repeated we had an open invitation to stay at his house in Travesia. He reiterated the town's name and the meaning of the word, which coincidentally is a long journey or crossing. Lucas's fishing boat suggestion panned out and we found ourselves a free ride on a crab boat named Bad Jack in really bad weather.

Roatan was just okay in our opinion. In 1997 there was only one dive shop, but large cruise ships arrived regularly and there were a few condos on West End. We stayed at the Wilson's ramshackle wooden hotel built off of their family home. Just like the nursery rhyme suggests, my life was but a dream, and now my dreams were starting to seem like a continuation of my waking life, just one subconscious loop endlessly running. Here, both my dreams and my waking reality became haunted like the Wilson's house. I think this is the only time I've ever experienced something like this, but I sensed a tortured woman's spirit. There was some sort of dark energy or abuse that had taken place there. I saw in my mind's eye a young girl, maybe seventeen years old, in an old fashion long sleeve cotton nightgown. She wandered the house at night, tormented, with the old wooden floorboards creaking. The dog they kept chained up under the porch, that was literally skin and bones, would begin barking and howling sometimes all night long. I lied awake wondering if the ghost had any interest in us and if the dog sensed her, too. *Was he just reacting to the creaky floorboards or was he barking out of pure starvation?* If I did sleep, my dreams were haunted by this place, and I was exhausted during the day.

I felt so bad for the dog. I told Jimmy we had to feed it. As we began to go under the house one day getting closer to the dog, Mr. Wilson yelled at us not to touch him. I became so upset, not just about how he clearly abused his animals (he also had a monkey tied to his mango tree), but because of this tormented girl as well. I completely lost it. I began yelling about how cruel he was, pointing out the fact that he worked in tourism and could not and should not torture animals in front of his guests. "People don't want to see you starve your dog and mistreat a monkey! You need to listen to what your paying customers are telling you!" He told us to mind our own business, and if we didn't like it, we should leave. I was so rattled, that's all I could talk about the rest of the day to our vendor friends. They were sympathetic and made suggestions as to where we could camp for less. Jimmy urged me to calm down since we still had a few more nights paid at the Wilson's, but the idea of actually leaving festered in my head. I knew I was on an emotional runaway train, but I couldn't get off. All I could do was mentally prepare for an inevitable crash. I jumped to future scenarios in my mind that involved us moving out, what else I should tell him about the mistreatment of animals, what he might tell me, how I would respond, and how I could really stick it to him.

That night, Jimmy's unwavering positivity led me by my hand, tip toeing up the stairs to our room as to avoid another confrontation. Surprisingly, we slept well and for the first time since we had arrived, we never heard the dog bark once. *Hmmm, maybe he had finally fed him?* I wanted to move out the following morning, but Jimmy insisted we wait and see what happens. That morning, Mr. Wilson grunted to greet us in passing, but then he did something remarkable. He apologized! He said he was sorry, but that I needed to realize that I was visiting another country. Not everyone treats their animals the same. And then we had an actual conversation. I agreed, but I also said he needed to be sensitive to his guests' feelings, and for God's sakes, if he was going to have a dog, *feed him*. It wouldn't take that much. So, there it was, right off the cuff.

It made no sense for me to be stuck in negative future thought patterns, ruminating over and planning what may never come to be. Now whenever I catch myself riding the rails of conflict or even find myself preparing to be charming, thinking of the funny little things I *might* have the opportunity to say in the future, I bring some humor in to let it all go. I imagine I'm in that runaway train, riding right by a huge Buddha statue. "Goodbye to trusting that everything will work out," I imagine myself saying as I wave to the only thing I know to be true (the present moment) passing by. As I see the Buddha go whizzing by in my mind, it is a visual reminder that I am now embarking on a journey that is taking me away from trust, and instead, I am consciously choosing to invest my energy in future ridiculousness that will probably never happen.

Chapter 16

Gettin' Freaky

Our timing was perfect for Reggae Sunsplash now. This could be our grand finale and then Miami was so close. We thought we might as well complete our circuit at my parents' house. Jimmy and I arrived in Puerto Cortes and got the cheapest hotel room we could find for $13 a night. We began to walk inside the shipping dock soliciting barges for a ride to Jamaica or if possible, directly to Miami because at this point our funds were so low, we needed to head back to U.S. soil and greater earning potential as soon as possible. In regular cities such as this, it was nearly impossible to sell our jewelry. Cortes was a blue-collar economy without much room for extras, so it was silly to even try. We stuck to the docks during the day and were careful not to be on the streets too late at night. One night while we were walking back to the hotel from dinner, we saw a large rat cross the street. A group of teenage boys were immediately on top of him, kicking this animal back and forth like a soccer ball laughing, yelling, and full of adrenaline. This was a good indication that our intuition was right. Cortes was definitely rough around the edges.

The crew members we spoke with told us that Jamaica was unlikely, as there were very few boats that traveled that route, and none were in port at the moment. Miami was a possibility, but most captains were hesitant to take on passengers, as boats were heavily policed and all crew members listed and checked upon arrival. We were also told Captains needed to be careful who they took on board because passengers could be carrying drugs, which put them at risk (sideways glance). Still, rumors of first-class dining halls and movies playing on a big screen television while at sea kept us motivated.

When we got down to our last fifty dollars, Jimmy suggested we leave the hotel to make sure we would still have enough money to eat. We decided to sleep inside the port gates in an empty shipping container. We felt it was somewhat safe as there was a security guard at the gate that we would pass by every day, never really sure if non-employees were supposed to enter. For that reason, we brought our things inside in the late afternoon and remained hidden within the gates the rest of the evening. It seemed as if other people had been doing the same thing. There was piss and shit in and around the containers. We chose the least dirty one and hunkered down for the night. I barely slept, scared we'd get robbed or worse. Admittedly, this was not what I had imagined for us. I hoped and prayed that things would somehow turn around.

The next morning, I decided to go to the local market. Jimmy would stay at the docks, and I would try to use machismo to my advantage, selling our jewelry at discounted prices. An older gentleman spoke to me for a long time and then eventually bought a pair of earrings for two dollars. Things were looking pretty bleak when a familiar face came into the market. I couldn't place him after meeting so many people on our journey, and once again was distracted by my own mind and needs. It was Lucas. He had to remind me that we had met in Puerto Cortes before, and he had invited me to stay at his family's home on the beach in the neighboring Garifuna village of Travesia.

Of course! Why had I completely forgotten about this option? Maybe because Lucas was extremely good looking and fit, possibly with ulterior motives, and I had a boyfriend? I told him all the details of our situation and explained if we went to stay with him, it would be myself *and* Jimmy, which he said wasn't a problem. We chatted a bit more, me thanking him for the Roatan fishing boat tip and him describing his art. He was a graphic artist and had lived with his mother in Los Angeles. He was working on a revolutionary new advertising product there, which he hoped to be the first to implement in Honduras. It was a two-toned billboard much like latticed window blinds with one advertisement that when turned, revealed the backside, which had a completely different image. Not that interesting to me, but the prospect of finding a free house to stay in on the beach was certainly exciting. We packed up to find Jimmy and make a move.

Lucas put us on a local bus, and he rode his bike back to the village. He had an acquaintance staying on his couch, Carter, a man who had recently got out of jail (I didn't ask). Lucas said we could sleep on the floor in the back bedroom, having it all to ourselves. The house was right across the street from the beach, and he used the neighbor's hand well for fresh water when she wasn't looking. That first night, as we attempted to sleep on top of our tarp and sheets on the hard cement floor, we heard African drumming coming from nearby in the jungle, all night long. In the morning, we had to ask and the two explained there was a nine-day Garifuna ritual taking place in a palapa (thatched hut) just down the road. Carter expressed his disapproval saying he thought it was wrong that they were sacrificing perfectly good animals. He disagreed, not out of sympathy for the animals, but because of all the hungry people in Honduras. "They offer that perfectly good meat to the spirits, just burying it on the beach and letting it rot." Lucas interjected that it wasn't just to "any spirits," divulging that they pay tribute to and are attempting to communicate with their dead ancestors. "You should go," he encouraged us. Carter shook his head no, laughing and said, "You will never catch me there again. That's just wrong and a bunch of hoodoo voodoo. I believe in the Bible, man."

We all went to the beach for a swim for the very first time. It was incredibly dirty, mostly with sticks, leaves and seeds, but also diapers and garbage as well. Carter pointed out where the dead cow was buried just up from the beach, which was one of the sacrifices. As we were all swimming, a boat with three guys stopped, hollering something in Garifuna language we couldn't understand. Lucas translated and said they were motoring to Belize to buy coke and marijuana if we wanted to join. It was just for a night or two. After questioning him more, he added it was probably safe. They would stay at some guy's mansion who Lucas knew and there was no port authority or immigration where they docked. As much as we would have loved to see Belize, and this was an opportunity knocking on our door, we declined not needing any more problems than we already had. Carter wanted in though and ran back to the house to get his wallet. He swam out to the boat in his underwear, with his t-shirt, jeans and wallet in one hand overhead. He was leaving with just the clothes on his back. We said goodbye, waving and wishing him luck. "See you in a few days, Carter!"

Night two, we were still too shy to check out the ritual, even with Lucas pressing. Day three, Lucas introduced us to some older Rastas who were living off the land, growing most of their own food. He suggested we buy a small piece of property from them in the jungle for three or four thousand dollars. Not exactly our budget or our mindset in that particular moment, but it was an interesting idea. Jimmy and I met some nice people on the beach. One woman lived in New York but she came back home every year for the "festival." She officially invited us to join, so now we had an in.

After we ate dinner, and shortly after we heard the drums start, we headed over and entered the jungle palapa. The men were drumming in the center of the circle, with the women dancing all around them. There were a few dead chickens hanging on the circular bamboo walls and a cow's head in a large pot to the side on the floor. The intensity of the drumming would build and tighten like a flexed muscle and then let go, becoming more relaxed. There was a woman, clearly inebriated, in some sort of a trance, spraying alcohol through her teeth into the crowd. As the music changed, so would the direction of the dance circle and the lyrics they were singing. We began to join in the dancing, but I couldn't help to feel we were in the way, clueless as to the changes of the movements. Then, when the trance lady spit her mist of alcohol right in my face, I definitely felt less than welcome. As the tension was building in the music again, I noticed a few women coming in with live chickens under their arms. One woman had a knife which I took as our cue to leave. I certainly didn't want to see anything being sacrificed. We moved naturally with the crowd and left out the doors on the opposite side of where we had entered.

"Hey! There you are! How you all doin'?" we heard from a familiar voice. It was our beach friend who had invited us, now swinging in the hammock. She was dressed in traditional clothing like many of the other women, in a ruffled white blouse with a red and yellow checkered skirt. "You all have to go in there," she said warmly. We were out of breath from dancing and the fear of witnessing a ritual sacrifice.

"We were in there, but we got scared. It looks like they are going to kill some chickens."

She reassured us that all the killing was done and that, "You [we] have to see this." With that, she got out of the hammock, grabbed a wandering chicken and joined the group. We told her we'd be in shortly. Jimmy agreed to take one last look with me before going back home to Lucas's. This time when we entered, the women were dancing *with* the chickens. As the music became faster and more intense, they would shake the chickens over their heads, which produced added harmony with their fearful gobbling. As the circle wound around, we saw our friend swinging her chicken wide from side to side between her legs. "Hi," she greeted us, smiling as she went by swinging her chicken in the air. We slowly made our way out of the palapa, listening and observing. I could feel the trance-like focused energy of the room which did seem was going elsewhere. But, because it was an unfamiliar energy, it was a little scary to me. I had no doubt, that they *were* communicating with something, or possibly someone on the other side. I didn't know if it was hoodoo or voodoo as Carter had said, but it wasn't anything I felt particularly called to.

Lucas wanted the details when we got back. We were glad we went but probably wouldn't go another night. Now, when we went to sleep, at least the mystery was solved. We knew what the drumming was and where it was coming from.

With the port now a bus ride away, we had put our cargo ship plans temporarily on hold. Jimmy was getting up early in the mornings and going for a swim at the beach. All the garbage made it less than appealing for me, so I preferred to sleep in on the concrete floor. One morning, I awoke to both a familiar yet unusual sensation. Jimmy was kissing my breasts, yet it didn't feel like Jimmy, and this wasn't something he would have felt comfortable doing in the morning, knowing it would most likely lead to rejection. Admittedly, I *was* still a bit of a prude, and rarely initiated sex myself, but would rather "allow" it every few *nights* or so. My eyes flew open and there was Lucas, laying alongside of me, sucking on my tit.

"What do you think you're doing?" I asked him.

"Gettin' freaky?" was his response as he released my nipple with a bounce. He wore a mischievous grin in an aren't-you-willing kind of question.

"Jimmy's right here at the beach! He'll be back any minute! Do you really think I'm going to have sex with you right now?" I demanded to know, shocked.

He muttered something about mutual attraction, but I knew I had never given him the impression that he was welcome in our bedroom while my boyfriend was away. By this time, I was used to managing male attention, both wanted and unwanted, but this was taking things way too far. It was seriously disturbing that he thought he could come into our bedroom while I was asleep and completely unsuspecting. I sat up, pulling the sheet over my chest, and I shook my head no, not budging. Defeated, he made his way out of the room.

Now this was uncomfortable. When Jimmy got back, I suggested we go into town to buy more rice and beans and try to call his parents to see if they could help us. I would have loved to stay in this part of the world, but it hardly seemed like an option for us anymore. This time, his dad agreed to a cash advance on Jimmy's Alaskan PDF (Permanent Dividend Fund). He would purchase us plane tickets back to Miami and wire the minimal amount of cash necessary for us to survive on and get ourselves to the airport. The phone call was so expensive we agreed that we better *walk* back to Travesia because even saving a dollar helped.

As we walked back, I began to tell Jimmy what had happened that morning. I didn't think it was necessary for the two of them to talk, or for Jimmy to create a riff since Lucas was the owner of the house we were staying in. But he was clearly upset. He considered Lucas a friend, and he not only thought what he did was sexual assault but also a violate of both of our trust. As we began to wear out the topic, we came to a long open stretch of road. There was a clearing to the left, and very poor housing dotted along the right. We saw a beautiful woman who looked like a Victoria's Secret model in a lace lined camisole standing outside of a cardboard shack. As we got closer, she slowly came into view more clearly. Her camisole was dirty and torn and when she smiled and greeted us, she covered her mouth with her hand to hide a number of missing teeth. We then realized that these people were all living in front of the garbage dump. Their houses were built and cluttered with found objects. This is probably the poorest area I've ever walked through in my life. Still, the people were friendly, and the children were curious, laughing as they ran in wide circles around us, kicking a deflated soccer ball down the road. The fact that not only this women's image had looked like a Victoria's Secret model but that her very *soul* could have actually been in the body of a celebrity, or within someone living as a dump dweller blew my mind.

Heavy questions came flooding in as to why we are born into certain circumstances. Hindus would say past life karma, which is an explanation that Christianity doesn't provide as to how God could allow so much suffering in the world. My white privilege was not lost on me in this moment. Sure, we were currently broke with no home passing through this space in time, but we were only passing through.

Our upbringing allowed us a lot more opportunities, and our parents were still providing a safety net, thankfully, to get us back home.

As we rounded the corner, the beach came into view and Lucas was riding his bike toward us. Apparently, the last bus had just arrived and since we weren't on it, he thought he better ride to town and check on us. That was very sweet, but still didn't excuse him from Jimmy's hurt, which he painfully described in an awkward lecture. Lucas first asked him if he wanted to fight, but eventually apologized to us both and reassured Jimmy that it shouldn't make things uncomfortable between us all. We shared hopeful information about possible flights and thought to finally get our passports stamped in Puerto Cortes if it was possible. When we got to the house Carter was back and the stories and weed from his adventure were welcomed distractions to take all of our minds off of the morning's event.

The following day, Lucas was still flirting with me, or possibly trying to be cute to make amends. Shirtless and incredibly hot, he was happily sweeping the house with his Walkman on using the broom like an air guitar. He looked me in the eyes as he sang out loud to Peter Tosh that only he could hear. "Lookin' at your crystal ball culture man...."[16] I laughed, shaking my head no. Cute, but still no. I stepped outside to be with Jimmy where he was sneaking a shower at the señoras well. I felt a sharp thorn in my heel as I walked amongst the garbage that like many of the local homes, was just thrown on the ground outside the door. As I reached down to pull it out, I realized

---

[16] Peter Tosh, "Crystal Ball", Track #4 on *The Toughest*, Capitol Records, 1988, vinyl

it was an intravenous needle. My hands were trembling as I removed the needle and Jimmy and I were both in tears as we presented it to Lucas demanding to know, "Why the fuck would you just throw a dirty needle outside on the ground?" In a panic he tried to explain.

"No, no, no, it's clean," he showed us the package which really didn't prove much. "I use them to clean my computer. See, I clean my computer with the air from these," he stammered, showing us the little hole the needle fit through. We really didn't know what to believe. I was in full tears, saying I would have to wait six months to get tested for HIV, which was rampant in Honduras. Lucas reassured us we had nothing to worry about, clearly feeling horrible. That was it. We had to get out of there. We went to see about our passports and call Jimmy's dad regarding progress on plane tickets the next day.

There were a lot of raised eyebrows at the immigration office. We had stamped into Guatemala on May 8th but never stamped out. Here we were in the month of July, in Honduras, with no evidence of how we got there. We didn't really believe in borders, so we hadn't realized this would be a big deal. Still smiling, we described our river crossing, which was received with lots of negative head shaking and unmet sympathy. They said this was a *grande problema* and they would have to talk to their supervisor. With that, our passports were gone. Upon return, we were told we would have to pay $50 each to solve this problem. We began to understand that it was the immigration officers that clearly didn't know who they were dealing with. We were obviously not rich gringos who they could extort $100 from. We explained pointing, "We, no dinero – you stamp pleeeasssee," with hands begging and knowing full well they had the capability to help us free of charge. Nope. They were going to have to keep our passports until we paid the fine. So be it, because this was no bluff, and we truly didn't have $100. It was on them that we were now walking the streets with no passports. Adios amigos. We moved forward to call Jimmy's dad.

We didn't bother with immigration again until we knew that money should be waiting for us at Western Union. When we did go back, we were adamant that it was impossible for us to pay $100, which now they believed. We offered them $20 for both and resolved the issue incredibly fast. Hallelujah! We were back to buses and Miami bound soon.

Chapter 17

#vanlife

My parents were relieved to see we were alive and well. And although contrived, it seemed we had turned a corner, a reverse psychology type of corner. I was glad there was less surface tension, and my parents were doing their best to not interfere with any of our future plan making. They had probably come to the realization that anything they warned me against, only produced the opposite effect. And after such an epic journey, I felt more convinced than ever that this was not just a phase but would somehow become a way of life for me. They set some boundaries, making it clear we were welcome to stay at their house for one month, but if we wanted to stay any longer, our way of life would need to include getting jobs. After having just spent six months traveling abroad, the suburbs of Miami didn't seem like an option for us.

We were jungle people now and taking full advantage of still being in the tropics we were foraging their suburban neighborhood for more natural materials, seeds and bamboo, the latter for Jimmy's flutes. And although it was not the same at all, in fact it was the opposite of what we were doing, which I *tried* to communicate, my mom insisted that she wanted to encourage Jimmy's flute making by buying him multiple tubes of white PVC. She was excited by the idea of taking us to a local flea market where Jimmy could have people color the plastic flutes she envisioned him making with magic markers. She thought it was a brilliant idea, and I became irritated with the whole thing. But Jimmy told me to just roll with it, saying that my mom was just trying to show us her love. We went to the flea market and were completely unsuccessful, but Jimmy continued to shine his light in and around my relationship with my family, telling me that my parents were, "The best ever." This was his go-to response for my mom's meals or anything that was presented to him for that matter. To this day, my mom will still reference Jimmy while laughing as she repeats his over-used phrase, "The best ever."

We looked into taking the Amtrak train back to the West Coast, but it was too expensive. When our thirty days were up, we boarded a California bound Greyhound bus and began heading to Alaska much like the way we had started; stopping at a few friend's houses, and then hitch hiking back to Idaho to meet up with Jimmy's family. As we started to move through the U.S. again, it became clear just how much our journey had impacted us. The subtleties of American culture that before we may have hardly noticed were magnified as we began to experience a type of reverse culture shock. The cut-throat nature of capitalism and materialism were even more blatant, as was the amount of excess. We had seen the happiness and resourcefulness of people who had far less, and here we saw people who were displeased when they had houses full, even garages and storage units full, of things they hardly ever used. This was all evidence to me that even though yes, money was proving to be necessary, I personally would never work that hard in the machine. I knew that I would always prefer to live a simpler life and not allow myself to become a slave to big toys such as sportscars, boats, jet skis and motorcycles. We had shed our skin, a thousand times over, having experienced so many new things and cultures. Now that we were back in California, it was strange to see that nothing with our friends had really changed. It was as if time had stood still while we were gone. Everyone was still smoking weed on the same couches, working the same jobs, and aside from a few weekend getaways, most hadn't experienced anything relatively new at all. Unintentionally, nearly all of my sentences started with, "In Guatemala…(fill in the blank)," but usually I was comparing the cost of everything, as we were now shocked by U.S. prices. It must have been super annoying because at one point a friend finally told me, "We are *not* in Guatemala."

Late November of 1997, exactly one year after we had left, we arrived back to Sutton, Alaska just in time for winter, the very thing I was trying to avoid the year before. We had arrived in Idaho at Jimmy's grandmother's after Thanksgiving and again, the six of us piled into his family's five passenger dually truck to make the journey all the way back up the Al-Can highway together. Jimmy was super excited to be back and spending time with his best friends, but after just a few days in the cabin, I felt even less welcome than before. Wyatt and Bailey now had two American Bull Dogs who were trained attack dogs to guard and protect their grow operation. They would have to drag the dogs barking and lunging at us into the bedroom or their outdoor pen where they

213

constantly barked. We used their bathroom and bong regularly, so it was quite an ordeal. I wondered what would happen if the dogs burst through the bedroom door. *Would they go straight for the jugular?* I started thinking about broadening our horizons, preferably sooner rather than later.

I loved being in nature, but compared to my suburban California upbringing, this was *very* remote. I had no friends here, no transportation, and we were thirty minutes from a grocery store. The snow was starting to pile up as well. Admittedly, I am an extrovert and would have liked to have *some* interaction with like-minded people or just *any* other people for that matter. I reminded Jimmy that he could earn good money working for his dad on Kodiak Island where there was more of a town and an actual community. I persisted that it would be a better environment for me. I could have actual conversations and walk to the supermarket and the local downtown area.

We alternated staying in the cabin and with Jimmy's family through Christmas. I did well selling my jewelry at the local holiday art fairs and was able to save some money. My new plan was to buy a vehicle that we could either use to get ourselves to and from the cabin or take over to Kodiak Island. Through the art shows, I finally made my own friend, Suzanne, a bad ass leather craftswoman who was raising her two kids alone in a cabin she had built herself about ten miles up the road from us. At one point the temperature dropped to twenty degrees below zero Fahrenheit where it stayed for many nights. It would warm up to zero during the short daylight hours. Wyatt and Bailey's goats and pigs were under fed in my opinion, which was just another thing that bothered me about them. When Wyatt held up their smallest goat, dead and frozen stiff from the cold one morning, laughing, that was the last straw for me. These were not my people. I wanted to go to the "banana belt" of Alaska.

Just before we left for Kodiak, I was able to buy Wyatt's dad's van, a beat-up old Chevrolet, fully gutted in the back for $600. He threw in a piece of ivory (a wooly mammoth tusk with scrimshaw etching) that he said was probably worth $200 as part of the deal. We put the van on the ferry to the island, and now I had wheels, just no driver's license. My next step would be to save enough money to clear my California driving record. I had lost my license due to a number of speeding tickets, and then ultimately a "failure to appear in court." With the computer systems now connected state-to-state, I needed $300 to eventually get myself an Alaskan driver's license. Jimmy drove it in the meantime, working as an electrician's journeyman assistant with his dad. His father rented us a small apartment next to James (his journeyman and Jimmy's co-worker) and his girlfriend Gloria. Every morning when Jimmy's alarm would go off at 7:00 a.m., he would resist getting up and complain about having to go to work. During the day I would hang out with Gloria, a thirty-six-year-old ex-Alaskan Bush Company (yes, it's a real place) dancer whose stage name was the Arctic Fox. She was a beautiful native woman with lots of stories to tell as well as a chronic weed smoker and an alcoholic. We would smoke pot, and I'd make jewelry to put on consignment in various shops downtown. Gloria was unmotivated. She would just sit and watch me, reliving her past and educating me about village life through her story telling.

Every few days I would walk through town, making my rounds to see if I had sold anything. I made a nice connection with all of the store owners. One woman who owned an Alaskan gallery and import store suggested that if I was looking for work, that I inquire at El Chicanos Mexican Restaurant. They were, "always hiring." Maybe I seemed a bit lost to her, but I wasn't actually looking for work, at least not as a waitress. I explained that I had worked in Arizona to fund Jimmy and my trip on the premise that he had a good paying job in Kodiak with his dad. At the moment I was fine with selling my art and him supporting us both until a job I was actually interested in came along, but I wasn't actively looking. "Okay," she shrugged looking puzzled. The next time I went in her shop I was surprised that she offered me a job, which was exactly what I was interested in. As a gallery, she sold artwork made by a number of local artists, as well as carried a variety of Alaskan made products from all over the state. As an import store, she sold greeting cards, fossils, crystals, incense and other beautiful hippie items. Debra made jewelry there herself as well, so when it was slow, she expected me to clean and create jewelry using her beads, stones and Swarovski crystals. She began to teach me new wire wrapping techniques and I learned more about art, gems, precious metals, and how to run a gallery/consignment shop. Though it didn't pay much, I was in heaven playing in someone else's bead collection and learning more about the things I loved. I could sell and promote my jewelry there as well, so it was a dream job for me. After a few days training with her, she gave me the keys to open myself so she could spend Saturday at home with her family. I had trouble unlocking the door my first morning, so I walked across the street to the payphone and called her to ask if there was a trick to the door. She explained how to lift, pull and push but said she would be there to help soon. I had already gotten inside when she pulled up with opera music blasting from NPR on her car radio. She parked, but the blaring opera continued to call attention to her as she used her rearview mirror to drop Visine in her eyes. *Hmmmmm*, I thought. *This could be the start of a beautiful relationship!* Debra was great, and she was indeed a pot smoker. I met a lot of people (especially local artists) through her and working at the store. I was beginning to settle into the Kodiak community.

At home, Jimmy's whining continued. He was like a child not wanting to go to school and somehow, I had assumed the role of the parent. On the mornings when it seemed he wasn't going to go to work at all, I had to go get James to come help me reason with him. Gloria would wait until payday so they could go out drinking to the point of violent belligerence and then involve Jimmy and I in their fights, usually in the middle of the night. They'd be on weekend bingers, and finally Gloria left the island mad, and James flew off after her. With James back on the mainland, Jimmy started to press me to follow suit. He wanted to move back to the cabin in The Valley where he could smoke pot and play music with his friends all day long. He would rather form a band and earn money making music. I had been there, done that, and was thoroughly enjoying the new life I was creating for myself. I was not leaving my job or the actual town of Kodiak to go back to Matanuska Valley where they proudly refer to themselves as *Valley Trash*. He was ready to move back, and I was ready to move on all together.

Nearly twenty-two, I lacked the communication skills to face what I knew would be a horribly dramatic and difficult breakup head on. So one day, in the midst of all his complaining and carrying on I agreed. I told him "Yes, fine. Why don't you go over there for a few weeks and get it out of your system? See what you think. Maybe you'll come back or maybe I'll go there, but just GO!" Then, once he was in The Valley and we spoke on the phone, I broke up with him. My reasoning was that he was clearly unhappy in Kodiak, and I liked it there. He didn't want to work, and I was happy with my job and the new friends I was making. He was back that night, on a last-minute flight, crying and pleading, promising me he would go to work and be responsible, but I knew he wouldn't be happy. It was actually more than that for me. I realized I wanted more overall than what he could give me, and I was done.

Before he left, we had been renting a room with a sauna on the basement level in a single mother's home. She was a bartender with three sons and her jaw would get going when she was cranked up on coke. This woman was more Jimmy's contact and friend. We weren't close at all. I always minded my own business there, just keeping to the basement. When we broke up, that ended the $250 rental agreement. I was making $400 a week, and rent was high, so I began house sitting and living out of my van, which I now had a license to drive.

I was probably one of very few eligible bachelorettes on the island at that time. I subsidized my income with dinner dates and spent at least one night on a boat with a Californian guy named Brian who was fishing for his second season. This was a whole different walk of shame in the morning. It required walking the harbor docks, which, at that time was actually the second largest fishing fleet in the U.S. That is to say, there were many boats, many men and plenty of witnesses. My dreads were a double-edged sword. The pro was that I had permanent bedhead, so as far as anyone knew, I could have been just running an early morning errand. The con, I was the *only* white woman (possibly person period) on the island with dreads, so not exactly inconspicuous. Brian told me he could get liquid acid once he was back home again, and though the relationship never became serious, he did send a vial in the mail later.

I bounced around house sitting for people with the little that I owned (mostly beads, books and clothes) in a few boxes in my van where I slept in between gigs. I began dating Gabe, who was exactly my age, something I really hadn't done since middle school. This was largely because I viewed guys my age as completely immature, and Gabe was not an exception to this. I was selling the liquid LSD through both of our contacts since Gabe had grown up on Kodiak. It was going for $10 a hit, which is quite expensive, seeing as though a vial was $75 to $100 at that time for about a hundred hits. Brian hadn't wanted any money for it either, so it was all profit. I had spent the previous weekend in my van at the Blue Grass Music Festival lighting people up, but was now pet sitting for a young couple who were recovering alcoholics/addicts. I had gotten the feeling that he was a bit controlling, reigning over her sobriety. Gabe and I had decided to drop and spent the night together at their house on Friday night. He just wanted one hit, and I took three drops on some sugar cubes. It was just starting to come on and we were still talking coherently about who else wanted to purchase over the weekend, when there was a knock on the door. The house was a downstairs rental underneath and on the backside of the main house perched on top of a hill that overlooked Kodiak town and harbor. I was housesitting for private people, and no one knew I was there. It seemed very unusual for someone to show up unannounced.

Gabe immediately began to get nervous, hiding in the alcove of the studio where the bed was tucked away. I brushed it off and cracked the door to see who it was. Two men. One whom I somewhat recognized, the other not at all. The blonde whom I recognized asked if I had any acid for sale. I was completely taken aback and physically recoiled. With my heart beating fast, "I don't know you, and I don't what you're talking about," was my slow, careful reply.

"You know me, remember? *The mushrooms* from the grocery store," he shined his flashlight on his face, and indeed, that was where I knew him from. He had been a bagger at the local Safeway grocery store and whenever Jimmy and I would buy mushrooms there, Jimmy would always joke and throw in a few winks about the regular mushrooms from the produce department. Things began to move in slow motion as he repeated, "Remember… from the grocery store," still holding up his light. This time, I saw a police badge in his hand, which I don't imagine he did actually show me. I was either intuiting that they were cops, starting to hallucinate, or hallucinating my intuition. I shook my head no and then by some divine intervention (because I would *never* think to say or do anything like this) I said, "It's late and this is a *quiet* neighborhood. You should go now." I closed and locked the door in their faces. I told Gabe what I saw, and he went from skeptical to nervous and then straight up paranoid. As he flip flopped around the apartment, waving his arms and moving in and out of every space, he had me replay the scenario a number of times. When I felt enough time had gone by, and they were probably gone, I poured the vile in the toilet and flushed. I threw away any other signs, the vial itself, the sugar cubes and the letter from Brian. Gabe began ranting about how all of this was my fault. He was calling me crazy, and actually accused me of being a witch. To the contrary, I felt incredibly calm in that moment and tried to reassure him that nothing was going to happen since I had destroyed all of the evidence. Nothing I was saying was reaching him, and he stormed out of the house, completely altering our plans by leaving me alone to trip on three hits of acid all by myself.

Even though I hardly cared, I had no time to process this before the phone rang. It was the housesitting straight-edge people. He had heard I was selling drugs out of his house and demanded to know what was going on. Thankfully the LSD wasn't very strong because this trip had absolutely taken an unexpected turn south. I lied and denied (a term the Arctic Fox had taught me), telling him his dog was fine and everything was going well. I suggested he talk to the upstairs neighbors, knowing they would give me a positively quiet review. He hung up to do just that and I received an apology phone call shortly after.

Finally, I could disconnect. I turned off the apartment lights and laid down on the couch. The moment I did, a bright light which I had assumed was one of the many downtown streetlights dimmed as if it was a spotlight on the house. Just as it went off completely, a short "whooop" of a police siren sounded. The police station was in direct line of site of the apartment. Now there was no doubt in my mind that they *were* undercover police officers that had come to the door, and I was being watched.

I don't know if I ever went to sleep that night. It was more like a meditative dream state. I could feel a mild electric charge in my physical body as I laid there with my eyes closed. Images of clouds, treetops, rainbows and light were sprinkled in senseless, dream-like thoughts. I got up in the morning to open the store. I walked the few blocks down to work in a long blue rayon hippie dress with waffled long underwear underneath for warmth and my twelve hole Pipi Longstocking boots on. I noticed a police car parked across the street from the shop. The officers watched me unlock the door and turn the lights on. After I sat behind the cash register at the jewelry making station, he pulled away. Absolutely no doubt.

I thought back to the night before and the badge. I doubted my mushroom friend had intentionally shown it to me. That would have cost him his job. He was obviously training because not too long ago he was a bagger at the local grocery store, *or was he? Maybe he was still a bagger but the only person who the cops knew that had any connection to me at all? Maybe he had felt bad, so he did actually show me something, or was emanating that message?* What Tucker had told me that night on the railroad tracks, years ago, the night of my O.B.E., came back to me in that moment. He had said that I would always know if I was going to be in danger. This was reassuring, because I was obviously continuing to be protected, but this event had shaken me up. The rumor back then was that you would be sentenced to ten years in jail for selling LSD, which prison was something I never wanted to experience. It just wasn't worth it.

A police car periodically passed by the shop for the next few days, but after that, things settled down and I purported to be normal.

Chapter 18

A Career?

Eventually, I found myself living at the road's end on Kodiak Island. In fact, that was the name of our neighboring roadhouse style Restaurant and Hotel. The population of the tiny community of Chiniak was fifty. Yes, 5-0! So not only was I living on an island in Alaska, but now I was living at the end of the road, a ninety-minute drive from town. As far as Kodiak goes, Chiniak is still accessible because it is connected to the road system. There are many villages in this large archipelago that are only reachable via boat or float plane. No longer working my gift shop job, I was living with my boyfriend Javier who was fifteen years my senior. Javier's appeal, besides being strong and handsome, was security. He was a good provider but had two small children that lived with him full time. He was taking care of me, but along with loving this man, I began providing love and care for his children who were five and six, all day long while he was at work. Javier owned an amazing post World War II property right across from the beach, which still had a cannon turret, Quonset huts (semi cylindrical corrugated steel structures), and underground bunkers on it. Plus, he had dreams. He had used the ex-military structures for various things throughout the years; grow rooms, a mechanic shop, and horse stables. But what he really wanted to do was convert them into guestrooms and build a tourist lodge. In this sense, I was getting closer to what I wanted for myself; living in nature with someone responsible and possibly building something together. However, the reality in that moment was that we were living in a very basic home that he was *planning* on slowly fixing up. It had running water via a garden hose in a makeshift kitchen and an outhouse in the back. For showers and laundry, we would walk the trail we had blazed to and from The Road's End.

Javier worked long hours on a construction site at the other roads end, near Fossil Beach, an hour in the opposite direction from the house. When he got home, he was usually too tired to work on his dream and we were all bidding for his attention. Instead, he smoked weed and drank beers. Occasionally, when he had too much to drink, he made a point of telling me that his kids would always come first in his life. This gave them (especially his daughter) a little too much leverage. During the day, the kids and I would play and make trips to open the little library as volunteers together, but in the evening, his daughter clung to her father and was no longer my friend.

My parents were planning their first visit to Alaska during this period of my life. They invited me to fly over to the mainland and join them for the majority of their trip. Our relationship was still strained, and though I did want to see them, and it would have been nice to share some of the beautiful places I had been in Alaska with them, it just seemed easier to stay and take care of Javier's kids. Javier had said he would find someone to watch them, but I didn't know how we would do spending two weeks in a car together. This did raise a small little red flag in my mind as a warning that I was now tethered to something that was *not* my responsibility, but it felt comfortable. Here I was in charge, and could be the adult-like, pot-smoking full expression of myself. If I were to go with them, I would be the child again, censored in the back seat. This meant I would only see them for a few days in Kodiak on the last part of their vacation. My parents came out to see us for the day and bore witness to what I considered to be a higher-class version of non-conformity. But for them, I was living in a shack, that *yes*, they agreed *did* have potential. I was learning to take their opinions less personally, and it was easy in this particular situation because I myself was unattached, knowing it was probably temporary.

While I could have been away, the kid's contracted the chickenpox, something that I had managed to escape all during my childhood. When my parent's saw me dabbing calamine lotion on their itchy spots, and them hanging on and breathing all over me, my mom warned me that it would probably catch up with me. Javier arranged for someone else to watch his spotted but healing children so that I could drive back to Kodiak to spend the last few days of my parents' trip with them hiking, fishing and seeing the town.

Shortly after they left, at twenty-three years old, I had an adult case of the chicken pox, which in and of itself wasn't that bad, but it seemed to tip the scale of my entire nervous system. Weeks after the last pock was gone, the skin on my face remained hot and blotchy, as an outward sign of something internally wrong. This forced me to take a deeper look within. I realized I had given up my freedom and was no longer being guided by the things *I* loved. I had stepped into someone else's dysfunctional dream, and I could feel the dis-ease of that, the misalignment and resentment rising like heat into my face. This unhealthy situation I had found myself in was manifesting itself, in what I was being diagnosed with as rosacea. I needed to leave. And I needed to generate something bigger and better for myself so I didn't have to continue living out of my van, which was hardly running anymore. I didn't want to depend on someone else in a relationship to survive.

I milled over my problems and career options with a Kodiak girlfriend on the phone. We were both getting energetically carried away by all of Javier's shortcomings, until she finally interjected making an excellent career suggestion that I had nearly forgotten about. She reminded me that when I had talked to her sister-in-law, I had been very interested in the recent therapeutic massage program she had attended but had not graduated from. She was right! I had always been drawn to the healing arts. How had I not thought of this?

My next trip to town, I spoke to this woman at length, and she lent me a book, *Massage: A Career at Your Fingertips*. I was super excited. This was definitely a viable career option for me as it was in alignment with my Mother Earth principle to heal and help the planet as well as others. Massage therapy would allow me to earn an income combining my interests in natural health, vegetarianism, herbs, crystal healing, and energy, all the while helping people. Plus, it was something I could take with me everywhere I went. I read the entire book including the school recommendations, and within a few days I had a solid daydream going which included studying in the state of Hawaii. Javier realized I was young and was being very supportive. I was becoming more and more excited, thinking that I had finally found a career path that made sense for me.

I pitched the idea to my parents who had eagerly been waiting for years to hear that I was ready to go back to school. They still had money set aside for my education, but this just wasn't what they had in mind. It was 1999, and massage therapy was just starting to gain momentum and some recognition in the medical community. I'm pretty sure I started off sharing the idea with my mom, but she quickly passed the phone over to my dad, not knowing how to respond to yet another one of my developments. His first reaction was, "Massage has sexual connotation." He asked why I wouldn't go back to school to become a teacher. "You are clearly good with children, and you could have the whole summer off to travel." I was surprised he still didn't know the answer to this. I didn't want to be a teacher because I hated the system. I had close teacher friends who complained there was hardly room for creativity anymore since they had to teach to test. I mentioned the school in Hawaii which was met with more resistance saying, "I'm not going to pay for a six month vacation for you in Hawaii even further away from us than you already are in Alaska." We ended on, "Life is not all fun and games, Michelle." A point that to this day we probably still don't see eye to eye on, as I believe that life is a gift and what you make of it.

We now had the Internet. In fact, I had been taking a computer class one night a week at the little library, and I had an email account under the nickname Javier had given me because of my dreads and tofu diet; Tofutti. In the days after our conversation, my dad had found the website of an accredited massage school in Gainesville, Florida where my sister was attending university. This would be our compromise. It wasn't Hawaii, but it was massage school. I began to adjust the daydream accordingly. I envisioned working in a resort or somewhere on a tropical Caribbean island post-graduation. I was quite pleased with myself really. I viewed this six-month, five-hundred-hour program as a career shortcut. During the last five years while the majority of my friends were studying at university, I had been spreading my wings and flying freely. Now, with this new skill set, it seemed I would be able to pass go, collect $200, and catch right back up to where they were in the game. Plus, I would be receiving free massages every day. Winner, winner!

Plans were being set into action. One of the prerequisites for the massage school was to receive three professional massages from different providers. Their reasoning behind this was, *how do you know you want to be a massage therapist if you have never received a professional massage before?* True enough in my case. They also wanted us to experience a wide range of treatments to explore various styles and levels of professionalism.

I received my first treatment from my friend Josie Cowler in downtown Kodiak. I loved her small space and low rent. She had cleverly used her own name for her practice so that every time she interacted with the public, old friends or new, she was always advertising her business. I completely enjoyed her treatment and throughout my training at massage school, her business model was what I held in my mind. For me, her office space was like white noise that remained somewhere in my mental background. When I thought about my future massage studio, I always referenced Josie's space. I appreciated the simplicity of her business and her ingenuity, having named it after herself.

Javier and I had clearly separated, but I left on good terms with him telling me if I ever needed anything, he would be there for me. I flew to Miami to spend the holidays with my family before massage school started in early January. When I first arrived, my parents were out of town. I laid in their big bathtub soaking in all the Epsom salts and bath oils I could find, along with what finally felt like self-purpose. I was resting in the water in this transitional state, knowing I was about to embark upon a huge step in this next phase of my journey. I didn't know what it would bring or if massage would be one hundred percent right for me, but I was ready to try on some sort of a career. I took my mom's sewing scissors and looking into their large mirror next to the tub, I began cutting my dreadlocks. The dreads I had thought I would keep forever, growing them down to the Earth as an extension of my pro-nature, anti-authority convictions. I had become tired of people pointing and staring at me, usually while I was stoned and paranoid in public. I was ready to be free from the radical label I had branded myself with and create a new avatar, one who flies under the radar. It would be a surprise Christmas gift to my parents as well, knowing my hair had been a huge source of embarrassment for them.

I snipped, snipped, snipped, going for a "cute pixie" look, leaving my wispy bangs in the front. But when I finished with the bath and washing my hair, I looked more like a matted guinea pig. My hair had been stuck in the same clumps together for over three years, and there it remained. I decided this was a job for a professional, so I took my parents' car and drove out to US 1 looking for a hair salon. I chose the first salon I saw, not realizing it was African American owned and operated with the same clientele. It would have been uncomfortable if I just turned around and walked out, so what the hell. I had embraced Jamaican culture with my dreads for years, so this was actually apropos. I was super emotional, not only about having cut all of my hair off, which was a huge part of my identity, but because of this horrible new look with my blotchy complexion. Therefore, all tact had flown out the window. I sat down in the woman's chair and both my despair and skepticism slipped out uncontrollably as I asked her, "Have you ever cut a white person's hair before?"

This was *not* the start of a beautiful long-term beautician/client relationship. This woman did not find any humor in my question. She pulled me up by the head, her comb twisting around my short hair. She turned to *all* of her colleagues repeating the question out loud, and then back to me responding, "Yes, I've cut a white person's hair before. Now, do you trust me or not cause you can just turn around and walk out that door." It was my chance, but now I felt fully committed and was afraid if I got up to leave, all the hair salon ladies might actually kick my ass. I apologized and explained the pixie look I wanted, and I also mentioned I had had dreadlocks, trying to point out that I indeed did respect black culture and also provide an explanation for the state of my hair. She got to work, quietly snipping.

and when she was finished, she asked what I thought. I hadn't seen myself with short hair (that was accompanied with a horrible perm) since the third grade, and she didn't leave any of my bangs long like I had asked. My face looked round, fat, red and blotchy. Not like a cute pixie at all. With all hopes for my new elfish identity crushed my reply was, "It looks like shit."

I know! Who says that? Not this woman's clients. She proceeded to verbalize *her* perspective.

"You came in here lookin' like that!" She demanded to know what exactly I expected her to do, "work miracles?" I slinked out of the chair in full agreeance, afraid she was going to beat me with her brush. She was right, I came in there looking like shit. I paid, tipped and walked briskly back to the car.

My mother was especially happy with this decision as I knew she would be. I, on the other hand, was still experiencing a bit of an identity crisis. I hadn't realized that by having short hair, combined with the masculine way I normally dressed, it would automatically qualify me for the gay dating market. Now I was clearly receiving more attention from women than men.

We all survived the hype and uncertainty around Y2K. My sister and I went to the three day New Year's Phish show together and partied "like it's 1999," which was the perfect send off to massage school. My parents helped me rent a cute little apartment within biking distance to the school, and on the first day, I knew that The Florida School of Massage was the right place for me. Upon arrival, we gathered in a large circle on the school grounds as part of a welcoming ceremony. After some opening words, the sixty-some new students faced one direction and the fifty-some old students the other. The owner of the school played the flute as we were guided through a Sufi ritual, placing one hand on each person's heart and one on their hand. We gazed into each other's eyes slowly, circling, and then moving to meet our next partner. Each new student connected deeply with a graduating student, intensely transmitting messages of love, knowledge, acceptance and occasionally nervousness or discomfort in our gaze.

Much of what I had experienced in my wanderings was built into or explained in the curriculum as we sat in chairs or sprawled out on the floor for lectures and massage demonstrations. In the beginning of the program, we took a quick quiz to determine what learning style we most resonate with; visual, auditory, reading/writing or kinesthetic. It was here (and only here where I've ever heard this discussed) that I realized I am a kinesthetic learner and that I learn best by *doing*, not via lectures, slide shows, reading or writing. Fireworks went off in my head. This explained so much. This was why I couldn't bear to sit behind a desk and listen to a lecture that nearly sounded like Charlie Brown's teacher speaking, "Wah wah wah wah," and why I felt like the only way I was going to learn about what interested me most was by throwing myself into the world at large. This was also an affirmation that studying something as hands on as massage therapy would absolutely be right for me. Because the staff knew that we all learned in different ways, they encouraged us to use whatever tools we saw fit to help us retain information. As an example, they said reading/writing and visual learners might be note takers, and auditory or kinesthetic learners may better absorb the information while drawing, knitting or working on a model plane (more fireworks).

Anatomy and Physiology was made fun with the use of longwinded, silly stories to help us remember the difficult Latin names for the bones and muscles such as describing Larry, the mechanic who was working on a car axel, pointing up to the car and exposing his armpit he said, "Axilla," or *axel Larry*. The hydrotherapy part of the program had a clothing optional area with a hot tub and a sauna. We were welcome to use it at lunch and before or after school. We discussed intention, energy and were led in group activities to explore trust and the power of unconditional touch. "Intention is everything," was a common phrase that teachers related to injury or life in general. An example of a minor sprain was used. "When we continue to ignore or isolate, the recovery time will be slow. It isn't until we begin to elevate, ice, and turn our attention or intention towards healing that the process accelerates. Whatever we choose to focus on, we move more energy into that area; be it our lives or our bodies." They emphasized how much change can occur when both the practitioner and the client begin to focus their energy on a certain area in the body. This spoke to me on a number of levels. I had personally seen that whenever I shifted my intention in life to a new direction, doors would open and energy would begin to flow to make that a reality. I had also seen that just like a chronic injury, the same lessons would continue to present themselves (be it trust, mindfulness, presence, etc.), until I acknowledged them, focusing my attention and intention to finally apply the knowledge to move forward in life.

They also taught us it wasn't our job to heal others. To this day, I cringe if I hear someone refer to themselves as a healer. Instead, they explained, "We are conductors, creating a space to allow healing to occur." They emphasized that ultimately everyone's health is their personal responsibility. The idea was that this approach also prevents us from taking on other people's energy. If we know that it isn't our responsibility to fix someone, then we needn't take people's problems or energy home with us. Much like a psychologist, the intention is to help people help themselves. By applying specific techniques to a localized area, we can help facilitate healing and greater awareness, but holistic factors (accident/ injury, rest, weight, diet, exercise, mindset, etc.) play a huge role in chronic pain and the body's ability to heal itself.

In addition to the 500-hour program, there were a variety of other classes that I enrolled in; Yoga, a Feldenkrais course, Transformational Voice and Intro to Vipassana Meditation. In Vipassana class, I learned more about Buddhist teachings and that my "Mother Earth Principle" was actually called *Right Livelihood*. This is one of the main principles taught in the Buddhist Eightfold Path (path/steps to enlightenment), which states that earning a living should be done in an ethical way. That we should not just prosper but do work that does no harm to others and brings personal fulfillment. The remaining seven principles are Right Understanding, Right Thought, Right Speech, Right Action, Right Effort, Right Mindfulness, and Right Concentration. Many of the lessons that had permeated into my life were finally being explained. Not only were mental fireworks going off for me, but I felt a huge sense of relief. *I was not a crazy person, and I had finally found my way to this information in an educational environment, HalleluJAH!*

I was receiving a well-rounded education, learning about energy work, reflexology, Shiatsu, Chinese and Ayurvedic medicine in addition to Western techniques such as; sports massage, connective tissue, Kinesiology and neuro-muscular therapy. The Eastern techniques were taught as a general introduction, and we spent more time on, and were encouraged to adopt a more Western approach which I was surprised to find myself gravitating towards as they explained more. The school warned against a "fluff and tuck" spa-style massage or finding yourself stuck in a fixed routine not variating from one formula. Their reasoning being to address what the client came to us for first and foremost and not get too attached to doing things "our way" or "one way," which again, made sense to me in life overall.

There was really only one thing I hadn't factored into my beat-the-system-and-receive-free-massages-every-day plan. I hadn't considered that the free massages I would be receiving would mostly be bad massages, awkwardly delivered as we all struggled to familiarize ourselves with the human body. Now I was limping through this wonderful experience with more aches and pains than I'd ever felt in my life; my physical body also assimilating the growth and transformation my mind and spirit were experiencing.

Within the first week of school, I had an older suitor, Kelly. True to his name he was effeminate with thinning long hair, and again, fifteen years my senior. We met at a party at the massage school, though he wasn't a student. I was reluctant to start a relationship with him as I was truly wanting to focus on school, and I viewed him as a young massage student predator. But Kelly was persistent, and he had amazing qualities. He had a great sense of humor, was very intelligent (in this introspective ecologist type of way), charming, and had a wonderful alternative lifestyle as an outdoor pot grower. Before long, we were in a very comfortable, supportive relationship. Through him I was introduced to the Northern Florida hippie community. Weekends we would go canoeing in the freshwater springs, camping, or to festivals. He would encourage me to spend time with the women in his circle of friends. I attended my first sister circles and moon ceremonies with them.

I was also working on trying to heal my relationship with my actual sister. We had fought growing up, and I had picked on her. But she also claimed that all the arguing that went on between my parents and I had ruined her childhood. I found that to be an overdramatization, as we had an above normal upbringing, until yes, my rebellion began. The arguments and my parents' worry started when I was fourteen and she was eleven. She admitted that we had both done the same things (sex, drugs and rock n' roll), but we had done them very differently, responding to the same parenting in opposite ways. Whereas I lashed out having an *external* reaction to their incredibly high standards, my sister *internalized* this, focusing on achievement and meeting their expectations. I threw myself on the front line, asking or debating to go away for the weekend with a boyfriend, to a party, a concert, etc. To avoid conflict, Amy would just straight lie or sneak around my parents to do all the same things. We discussed all of this, and I thoroughly apologized. So, in my eyes, the only thing left to do was to just keep plugging along, trying to make amends via an actual relationship. I regularly invited her to join the drum circles I was attending, to come canoeing with Kelly and I, to see live music, and a plethora of other activities, but she was hardly receptive. I took that as I sign that she was not ready to move on.

I had imagined my relationship with Kelly would be short-lived, and I'd be moving on to the tropics somewhere after school. We had both enjoyed Utila, Honduras in the past, so for my spring break he bought us tickets to return together. This time around I visited the Mayan ruins in Copan, and I did actually scuba dive, enrolling in an open water course while he actively looked for land. Kelly was interested in investing in a piece of property somewhere and starting a community with like-minded people. The single most compelling piece we saw was $8 a square meter, which was a thousand square meters with an ocean view and a well for only $8,000. We discussed him purchasing it, and I was all for it. I could envision having a hostel or a house and a garden where I gave massage treatments. But living in, much less being the camp counselor of an alternative community, was not my dream. I think Kelly was hoping to find something that fit into a future together so neither of those visions came into being there, at least not for us.

Talking about my experiences in Alaska had piqued his interest. It was one of only two states that he had not been to. Since I still had my van and personal belongings there, he asked why we didn't return to The Last Frontier together, at least for the summer. We could travel the state in my van, and then he would need to return to Florida for the grow season. *Hmmmmm maybe because I had already done that many times now, and I thought to move somewhere warm?* This invitation prompted a new inquiry. *How would I know when to listen to my inner voice and how to maintain enough awareness and flexibility to change the course, especially if the Universe was sending me another opportunity?* I didn't want to alter or put my life plans on hold for someone else again, but as Kelly pointed out, I *would* need to return to Alaska to deal with my van and personal belongings some time. He was making the decision easy, as he had the money to travel and was super excited about seeing more of Alaska together. Before long, I was swept up in the current of Kelly's enthusiasm. We were getting along swimmingly, and the more I told him about the natural beauty of the state and it's cultural nuances, the more involved I became in the planning as well.

Chapter 19

Low Hum

After my graduation from massage school in June, we flew to Kodiak Island to spend time with my friends and recover my van. Josie the massage therapist was one of the first people I organically ran into shortly after we arrived. Always positive, she shared her excitement of her upcoming wedding to the man of her dreams. She was planning on moving off island and asked if I would be interested in taking over her massage practice. Wow! This was an amazing opportunity, and of course the idea of an office like hers had constantly been buzzing around as a "low hum" in my organism all during massage school. I hadn't expected this actual office space would be presented or that I would be living in Alaska during the winter again. I asked her for more details and her date of departure, plus time to discuss with Kelly. She suggested I come by the office to have a meeting so she could explain what the offer entailed. She wasn't charging anything for the business, which included the office lease, her client list and phone number. She just had one stipulation.

Highly interested in stepping into a running practice right out of school, I discussed the possibility with Kelly. It would involve shortening our travel plans on the mainland to return to Kodiak which was never really the idea. Neither one of us had expected I would be anchored there again, but he was super supportive and agreed this was an excellent opportunity. In contrast to Gainesville, where because of the massage school, you couldn't throw a stone without hitting a massage therapist, the market was wide open on Kodiak Island. There was a Thai/Shiatsu practitioner as well as an acupuncturist on the island at that time, but Josie was the only full-time western massage therapist. I met with her in my dream office setting. She expressed she was happy to turn over her entire practice to me (noting she should probably receive a massage first) and that all she was asking in return was that I honored her massage gift certificates which she still had floating around unredeemed. She added they were all from Christmas with a one-year expiration date on them. She had eleven still in circulation and of those she suspected *maybe* four or five would still come in. I agreed to take over her business. This was too good of an opportunity for me to pass up. For her, I had arrived just in the nick of time and could almost seamlessly take over her practice. For me, as a recent massage graduate, this was nearly unheard of. I'd instantly be the owner of a successfully operating massage business at literally no cost. This was probably what had been calling me back to Alaska, and the deal just kept on getting better. She was leaving the next day for the mainland and offered Kelly and I her house to stay in while she was away and an invitation to her wedding, which was added into our travel plans.

Her office remained closed while we were both gone. Kelly and I began our trip on mainland, but eventually we took the van to Skagway and Haines on the ferry, places that were new to me. Kelly was an environmentalist through and through. For him, seeing Alaska was putting a picture to all of the books he had read by well-known historians and naturalists like Georg Wilhelm Steller. Stellar was a pioneer of Russia and Alaska. In fact, he, along with Vitus Bering (yes, of the Bering Sea) were the first non-Natives to set foot on Alaskan soil. Kelly loved reading their descriptions of North American plants and animals in these books that were written in the 1740's. I learned from his chatter about the Stellar sea lion, Steller jay and eider being his most notable contributions. He attempted to teach me about his heroes, citing Edward Abbey and Henry David Thoreau. I loved nature and considered myself an environmentalist, but I couldn't find the same passion for reading such old-timey literature.

When my van began smoking and guzzling quarts of oil daily, we environmentalists knew that was not okay. We finally blew a gasket in the town of North Pole where yes, of course, Santa's house *is* actually located. We decided to leave it at the mechanics where Kelly bought a newer and larger van from the same man. Here we easily converted our lives into this more spacious, nicer home. When we returned to Kodiak Island, we had incredible luck renting a small cabin situated on a private road between both a lake and the ocean. The friend who had been renting there left us his handmade kayak to use, which was perfect for Kelly, even though the quality and craftsmanship seemed questionable.

My new business not only provided a viable income but also something more valuable to trade, upping my barter game. I was able to trade my massage services for regular acupuncture, hypnotherapy, shiatsu, Thai Massage, chiropractic care and even prescription eyeglasses. Prior to massage school, I could (and normally would) smoke pot all day, every day. It was just "my norm." Now, putting my hands on the general public, I felt way more confident sober. Weed was great if I wanted to get creative, be outdoors or even clean the house. Though if I was being completely honest with myself, at times it would make me paranoid, twitchy or clumsy. I wanted to be at my best with my new clients, so I vowed to only smoke pot in the evenings after work or on my days off. Shortly after that I also told myself I would no longer spend time looking to buy weed. If it came to me or an opportunity arose to purchase it, great, but I no longer wanted to spend my time actively tracking down a bag.

There was a time warp that would always occur starting in the days prior to running out of weed when I would begin to panic and start focusing on locating more. I'd spend whole days making phone calls and repeatedly bothering people. Meanwhile, I might drive over to another friend's house, find out they had nothing for sale but get stoned off their personal stash. After, I would feel obligated to hang out and do nothing there for at least an hour or two so they wouldn't think I was using them for their weed. Then when a $60 eighth finally was located, it would usually look light and might only last a matter of days, depending on how many people I had spent time with or felt I needed to repay the favor. This was a continuous cycle, a big expense and a total time suck. By cutting this out of my life, I had more time for meaningful relationships, to explore new trails, climb mountain tops, and pursue other creative endeavors.

While I happily settled into work and networking, Kelly adjusted his Florida canoeing skills to cold water kayaking and began to paint large Haida-style totem art. He was also focusing his energy on the upcoming Gore versus Bush presidential election. I still refused to watch television, especially the news. But Al Gore, the democrat candidate was an environmentalist, which piqued Kelly's interest and consequently had him on the roof adjusting the rabbit ears to tune in the boxy black and white television set that came with the cabin. He was encouraging me to do something called a *Nader Trader* online. As a liberal-minded person, my individual (popular) vote would not count in the state of Alaska because it is a majority republican state. This was all being brought to light in the media, in addition to the fact that Ralph Nader's (the green party candidate) popularity could possibly divide voters and ruin Al Gore's chances of winning. Becoming a *Nader Trader* was a way to swap votes with someone from a swing state. They would vote for Gore where it could actually make a difference, and I would vote for Nader to help get the Green Party 5% of the popular vote, which was needed to qualify them as a legitimate presidential party to receive federal funding. All of this excited Kelly, but for me it just magnified the fact that America is not a true democracy. While we were so busy as a nation instilling democracy in other countries, which often was bullying or meddling in foreign affairs (usually in oil rich nations), we had the same non-democratic issues at home. The day of the election, there were traffic blockades and what was called, "wrongful purging of registered voters," which was mostly targeted at African Americans in Jeb Bush's (George's brother's) jurisdiction. I was becoming unraveled. I was shocked people could so easily overlook this larger global hypocrisy and became even more set on saving to travel again or possibly living abroad.

I was coming home from my first real weeks of work, doing four or five hours of massage a day completely exhausted, hungry, and in need of a massage myself. Kelly would normally be painting and/or watching television in the unkept cabin. I began to ask him to help out more around the house and be sensitive to the fact that when I came home after 7:00 p.m., I was going to be hungry. He was usually very receptive, but on one of the days I felt I needed more support, he wasn't home when I arrived. I was hangry and cooking once again when he finally came home with a story of nearly drowning in the cold Alaskan waters when the kayak began to split at the seams. I was too hungry and annoyed to be sympathetic about him almost dying, and as often happens, this one small thing led to a greater discussion. This was evidence for him that he should return to Florida. Winter was upon us. His one passion, paddling, was now too dangerous, and he was missing his close community of friends back home. Leaving my new massage practice was not an option for me. This internal message was loud and clear. I was really enjoying my new role as a local business owner and being part of the small wellness community on the island.

Kodiak is a very blue-collar town full of fishermen and "Coasties," hosting the largest Coast Guard base in the nation. As my acupuncturist friend pointed out, the island was not a spiritual vortex, but more of a "root chakra" type of place. Very earthy, very grounded, and centered around basic needs such as food, water, shelter, and safety. Not at all a heart based, third eye, Kundalini awakening type of place. There is a small artist and musician community, most of whom I was friends with, and now I was getting to know the alternative healthcare providers via trades and get-togethers. To gain more knowledge about the human body, I had just enrolled myself in an anatomy class at the local community college. For Kelly, Kodiak was lacking the widespread open-minded hippie culture he was used to, but I was happy here, and for me, I had found my niche. Hiking and beachcombing were my favorite pastimes, and we had a private beach with lots of sea glass right in front of our little cabin.

Kelly was ready to start a family, but I still wanted to travel more. His solution was, "Okay, so let's go travel," which just felt rushed, or like bad timing, as I was now concentrating on my brand-new business and couldn't promise a family. It was obvious we were in two very different stages of life. He made plans to go back to Florida before Christmas, and I decided to stay until February to take advantage of Christmas gift certificate sales (as Josie had highly recommended) and be responsible about delivering that service to people after the holidays. We would meet up in Florida in February, which we did, but by then I had already decided to move forward making a ten-year rule for myself. *No more dating men more than ten years older than me. They were in a completely different place in their lives.* I would aim to find someone who was responsible but still had a sense of adventure and was willing to explore with me.

Chapter 20

Can't Judge a Book

I knew that you, "can't judge a book by its cover," in the obvious sense, and we shouldn't make negative assumptions about people based on their outward appearances. But I have the tendency to make *positive* assumptions, which I know, are still assumptions. I'm just now beginning to wrap my head around the fact that someone could look like a hippie, do hippie-like things, even have a little hippie house, but actually still adhere to mainstream belief systems or worse, be a wolf in sheep's clothing. Riley was good looking with long hair, and he grew weed and brewed his own beer. He loved the outdoors, hosted regular sauna gatherings at his house, and played guitar. Plus, he was only five years my senior, so he fit within my ten year rule. I assumed because of his outward appearance that he would share my same ideology.

We had met years earlier, when I was working for Debra. He had asked me out on a date back then, and I was interested in and attracted to him, but because I had a boyfriend at that time, I had declined. Now that our paths had crossed again on the island, and we were both single, we decided to give dating a try. I learned early on that Riley was Christian and though we both knew his faith and my aversion to organized anything could definitely be a deal breaker, attraction and optimism propelled us forward regardless. He made it very clear on several occasions that Jesus Christ was his savior, and his religion was important to him. I, on the other hand, was now trying to read *Yoga Sutras of Patanjali*, attending yoga classes three times a week, starting to meditate more regularly, and continuing to cultivate conscious awareness to be a kind and loving person. We may have both looked the other way because I was raised Christian, did believe in God, and at one time had accepted JC to be my savior, but since then, my beliefs had expanded beyond just one way to God. I argued that I didn't believe we needed church to connect with the Creator or Universal Life Force. I pointed out how the basis of Christianity, which was love, may have actually been tainted as a dogmatic attempt to create law and order. Riley would concur with many of the points I made, but it was clear he was not going to abandon his faith. Furthermore, he viewed my lack of commitment to any one belief system as weak and indecisive. After each emotionally charged debate, we would end up giving our relationship a rest for a few days. We found if we just ignored the elephant in the room and focused on hiking, camping, music shows, weed and sex (yes, the sex that I was finally completely enjoying), we'd be fine for a while.

This theme continued to present itself time and time again. As obvious as it seems now that I should *not* have been in a relationship with a fundamental Christian, at that time it was incomprehensible to me that this outwardly adventurous person could possibly be so rigid internally. He wanted to save me, and I became obsessed with opening his mind. I pestered him to go to yoga class with me, which he refused. He tried sitting in meditation with me once when I told him praying is talking to God, and meditation is listening to God, which he said didn't do much for him. My ultimate goal was to get him to travel with me. We talked about going to Tikal together, the ancient temples in Guatemala. I just knew if he were to be immersed in another culture, he'd see an entire civilization (like the Mayans) couldn't be wrong. It was my hope that travel would open his eyes to diversity and letting go of one way.

We had been trying to make a go of this for nearly nine months. We cared deeply for one another, and for the first time, I felt like the timing of this could be right. We were both here in the same geographical location and in the same place in our lives; half rooted and half ready for the next adventure, which could possibly be marriage or a family together. There was only this one obstacle, but it was huge, and though we both wanted to overcome it, we couldn't see how.

He wanted me to hold his values in the same esteem, urging me to go to church with him, and I was constantly seeking validation for the things I believed in, including my career path. During one of our circular discussions, Riley told me that, "Massage is like taking echinacea. You're going to get better in a few days no matter what you do." This was a low blow. His lack of belief in massage translated to a lack of belief in *me*. Something that had been building up inside of me finally broke. I began sobbing. He held me as I cried, and he tried to convince me that his belief about massage or echinacea in no way changed how he felt about me as a person. But this did not register, as it was no longer just about us. It was my family dynamic all over again. It was structure verses freedom, and the familiar feeling of frustration that what I have chosen for my life is "unacceptable" and somehow not valid. *This* was what was causing all my emotions to come bubbling to the surface.

It is said we often chose partners that have the same energy as our parents, possibly because it is what we have known so we are able to interact in a familiar way, or in some cases, to work out unresolved issues from our childhood. In the past, friends had been perplexed by the significantly older men I was dating, and more than once, had dropped the term *daddy issues* on me. But back then, I really didn't think it applied. Sure, these men had provided a greater sense of security for me, but I had that with my father. I now knew that my main issue with *both* of my parents was their disapproval, which I translated as a lack of belief in me. I was coming into my mid-twenties, and I realized that I was still longing for their approval. I wanted them to acknowledge that even though my free-spirited way of life was a path less traveled, it was a legitimate way to move through the world. I wanted them to be proud of me. Riley and I had both chosen to live alternative lifestyles in the sense that we both lived in a remote part of Alaska, away from our families, but he had repeatedly dismissed my esoteric belief system, and now my career, making me feel as if I was null and void.

We began getting dizzy going around in circles. I went to church with him once, which only made matters worse. I left in tears, feeling like a sinner, questioning the many things he indulged in which his congregation preached against; premarital sex, cursing, alcohol and "drugs." We broke up, and then both of us were miserable, so we got back together again. I was probably driving my girlfriends crazy by constantly lamenting about this insurmountable barrier and whining about just wanting to travel again open-endedly.

The day Riley finally agreed to travel with me, it seemed all of my pressuring someone to do something they didn't want to and ignoring the inevitable truth may have actually paid off. He talked about making some repairs and improvements to his house so that he could possibly rent it while we were gone, enabling him to pay his mortgage and to provide a tiny bit of income. He would take some time off but would need to continue to work online. I wanted to accelerate the process, so I volunteered to help with any home improvement projects. One weekend, we were in his front yard with survey equipment, measuring and masterminding how to solve a drainage issue he was having. I had used survey equipment before to help Javier dig what-would-be his septic system out in Chiniak, so I was actually familiar with the equipment and knew the ideal slope gradient. Besides, it doesn't take an expert to know that shit doesn't flow uphill, and before long, we got into an argument. According to me, he would obviously have to reroute the pipe around an obstacle in the yard. When he did not agree, we could no longer move forward, and all of my validation issues came to a head. There was nothing esoteric about this. It was something I had experience with and could see clearly, yet he still didn't believe me. It made no sense for me to continue digging, if in fact, our current course was rising in elevation. I became super frustrated, pointing out the obvious fact that I didn't need to be at his house digging a trench with a shovel. His to-do list was a mile long, fall was upon us, and I highly doubted he would have his house ready to shove off anytime soon. I was done! I threw down the shovel, gathered my belongings I kept at his house, and was outta' there, for good.

This was our worst breakup yet. It felt as if it was really over, and none of our (my) validation issues were resolved. My heart, along with my hope for a serious future together, were crumbling into thousands of pieces. I cried for days, and then when I had to go to work, I cried at night. I couldn't sleep. My insomnia got so bad that when I would finally start to feel myself going to sleep, I would be so grateful that I would wake myself up with the excitement of knowing I was actually sleeping. With time, the pain began to lessen, and the old male to female Alaskan ratio helped to distract me from my grief (and myself) as I began to date again.

The next (Ethan) was a kayak guide in the summer and an extreme heli-ski guide in the winter. We were off to a sizzling start of a romance. He was good looking, open minded and adventurous, so we booked tickets to spend the month of April together in Thailand. He left the island to spend Christmas with his family and time at home in Washington State. Once he was gone, April seemed like a lonnnggg ways away. I began to get lonely and started wavering. I was planning on taking a massage course and traveling the West Coast visiting old friends for three weeks before Thailand. A week before I was due to fly to the lower forty-eight, I had to tell Ethan I could no longer travel with him. Riley and I were back together, ugggghhhhh. I felt horrible canceling on him. I knew a relationship with Ethan was a lot more promising, but somehow, I had gotten sucked back into the familiar energy of wanting to prove myself in this relationship. Ethan suggested we just meet there and then we could travel on our separate ways, but I knew that wouldn't happen. He ended up canceling his ticket and I went into a full-blown panic attack, as I thought about leaving the island all alone for the first time in over a year. I was overthinking the drive through Seattle traffic in a rental car (no smart phones or navigation still) and then going to Thailand all by myself.

The day before my flight, I had a fever and was physically trembling on my friend's massage table. She suggested I go to the doctor and get a letter stating I couldn't travel due to illness so I wouldn't lose my ticket. I received a massage, brushed off her suggestion and went home to rest. I was doubled over in pain. I had a fever, my stomach was in knots, and I was short of breath. I called Riley and told him I couldn't breathe. He said to breathe into a paper bag because I was probably hyperventilating. That actually did help and when he came over to check on me, I was starting to calm down. He told me I didn't need to go, but I knew I did. I wouldn't allow myself to become so fearful that I hardly ever left The Rock (Kodiak's nickname), which was a common phenomenon on the island, or in Alaska in general.

Once I was in the Seattle area, I managed to drive myself back and forth from a friend's house to a multiple day prenatal massage course in the city with no problem. I was sick with a horrible cold, but I did it. I was there. I drove down the coast, visiting the places and friends that I hadn't seen in nearly four years, and by the time I arrived at the Los Angeles airport, I was able to convince my nerves that I was just *excited* about going to Thailand on my own. It helped that my guy friends marveled at my bravery and were being totally immature about *BangKOK* and the lack of toilet paper in the country. I was going to arrive there at 2:00 a.m., so I booked one night at a hotel near the airport, which the Lonely Planet guidebook recommended. From there, I had no plans, and nothing was on the Internet the way it is today. My only hunch was to go to Chang Mai in the north to study Thai Massage.

Within the first 24 hours, I was in love with travel again. Koa San Road was a cultural circus with a plethora of lights, restaurants, street vendors, massage parlors and prostitutes. I spent a few days there slurping up curries, touring temples and then getting my wallet stolen in the marketplace. Luckily, I had stored a few hundred dollars and my one and only emergency credit card with a $1,000 limit in the locker at my guesthouse. It would have to get me through the month, and with $2 Shrimp Pad Thai, I didn't see a real problem. I was okay with making do. In fact, I actually preferred it.

Having come from winter in Alaska, I made the decision to go south toward the beaches first and then maybe to Chang Mai. Soon after, I was riding the rails to not-really-sure-where. I had a few beaches in mind, and since it was an overnight train, there was plenty of time to decide. I met a couple of American guys who were partying on board that were headed to the full moon party in Koh Phangan. They were insistent I should join them and by the time we disembarked in Surat Thani, I had agreed to ferry to the island with them. It was their second time in Haad Rin, so I followed their lead and rented a private cabin directly over the sea for $6 a night.

I was happy to experience the full moon party, but it didn't turn out to be "my thing." It was lots of trance music, mostly alcohol and some drugs (which no one offered to me). The guys were nice and tried to include me in a few outings, but I kept to myself and eventually found a Thai Massage course there on the island. I moved closer to town where the small open-air studio was and now had school to go to during the day. In the evening, I found a small bar with a good looking guitarist who was playing some of my favorite classic rock. When I heard him playing Bob Dylan and The Dead's "Gotta Serve Somebody," I felt called to introduce myself. He was a gorgeous long haired Spaniard named Matías, and when I finished my course, we began to travel together. He was from the Cannery Islands but had spent a lot of time in Hawaii and at Rainbow Gatherings in the States. We had similar interests with our paths nearly crossing at the gatherings which provided plenty of connection and conversation.

One evening in Koh Phi Phi while Matías and I were watching the sunset, I panicked, not having my camera to capture the reds and pinks of the incredibly beautiful sky. He stopped me and pulled me close to him saying there was no rush. There would be another and another and another. In fact, there was no chance of rain for months. I breathed a sigh of relief and relaxed into enjoying the present moment. I realized he was right, and now I saw the profound contrast of where I had been living. I explained that in Alaska the weather was pretty much guaranteed to be cold and rainy. "And why is it you're going back to Alaska?" he asked, casting the idea of my staying out into the open. It was tempting, as spending time with Matías felt really good. We shared a similar mindset, and I had nothing to prove to him. There was still snow on the ground in Alaska, but Riley had e-mailed me that the weather was unseasonably warm at the moment. It was definitely not barefoot bikini weather, but that was where I had built a life for myself, at least for the moment. That was where I needed to return in order to regroup and save for my next adventure. Thanks to Matías, a career vagabond, I now knew that perpetual paradise with a partner was a viable option.

After a sixteen-hour journey, which included a layover in Taipei, Taiwan, I was once again lying in bed with Riley. I had been gone nearly two months, and now, while catching up during after play, he told me he had remained faithful to me. I couldn't lie, so I was silent which was a message in and of itself. We never talked about it, but I know that moment of silence is what kept us from ever being romantic again. That, and the ease of Matías, which helped me get my groove back and realize there are a lot more open-minded fish in the sea, just maybe not around this particular island.

Over the course of the next few days, Riley and I swapped travel stories as he *had* actually gone to Tikal for a short stint. I was cautious about not saying too much about my trip, afraid that my sentences would start with "we." Mostly ears, and super curious to hear if he had drawn any alternative conclusions, I asked about his take on the Mayan culture and their disappearing civilization. I basically wanted to know if he thought the Mayans went to hell after they disappeared. The only thing he could offer me was that he would like to think God would have mercy on them if they hadn't been exposed to Christianity. Basically, it wasn't their fault if they had never been introduced to the idea of Jesus Christ, so there may be some sliver of hope for them at the gates of heaven. I had to laugh out loud. "Really! That was your realization?" I just shook my head. There was no point in having a discussion. He was too indoctrinated with man's rib, original sin and a white bearded man in the sky judging over everything. He was content and had no desire to expand his faith or grow beyond what he had originally been taught, even after having experienced sexual misconduct *firsthand* by his pastor *in his own family*. He was still unwilling to question or to think for himself, and I knew I would be moving on for good.

I went on one or two dates with someone from yoga class, but for the most part, I was now focusing on work, art and friendships. I was making seaweed baskets from the long ropes of bull kelp I would find on the beach, plus batiking and tie-dying up a storm. I didn't necessarily see massage therapy as a be-all and end-all occupation for myself, so when I heard there was a midwife on the island, I reached out to her. I was curious to learn more about midwifery, experience the miracle of life, and see if this wasn't something I'd like to pursue myself. I offered my new prenatal massage services for her expecting mothers completely free of charge for the opportunity to assist at a home birth. I also began to volunteer at the senior citizens center, giving them massages once a week. My cabin had been converted into an art studio, and I was on call to be present at a home birth and two hospital births for my friends. Life was good, but the weather still sucked, and I wanted to see more of the world.

Chapter 21

NDE Near Death Experience

Even though I had a newfound sense of responsibility, I was still addicted to altered states. I loved leaving the monotony of everyday life behind, but I was now beginning to rely less on the use of weed and psychedelics, and look more to travel, yoga, art, massage or meditation to induce a blissful state. At twenty-six years old, I still spent much of my time trying to remain on the spiritual plane unaffected by trivial matters. Now through massage therapy, I was able to give this gift to others by transporting them to an altered state via deep relaxation. This was the state I preferred to be in; relaxed and carefree; creating, stretching, biking, hiking, or traveling, unincumbered by day-to-day tasks.

I had made a decision to travel and live abroad indefinitely with no job and no solid plan, but this time with a career as a massage therapist and a few thousand dollars saved. I sold my car and gave up my rustic lakeside/ oceanfront cabin, as well as my downtown massage studio. I put all my belongings in a storage space on Kodiak

Island and vowed to spend at least a year abroad working or volunteering to help fund my trip. The year was 2002, and Work Away or Volunteer Tourism was not yet a thing. I thought to possibly transverse South America, starting in Ecuador.

I had operated the massage practice for over two years now, and my wrists and hands were starting to get tired. Larger people wanted more pressure than I could physically deliver, so a friend suggested I learn Ashiatsu, where with the use of bars on the ceiling, I could actually walk on people. My trip started in Florida with family and then in Tampa at an Ashiatsu Oriental Bar Therapy workshop. After New Year's, I went to Puerto Rico where I stayed with my great aunt and uncle. I hitch hiked a bit on my own to see more of the island, which probably was not the best idea with all the cat-calling Puerto Rican drivers. But it made me feel alive, throwing myself back into the unknown again. One day, while alongside the highway, a good looking North American man with long flowing blonde hair pulled over in a red convertible. Madonna's lyrics, "I fell in love with a beautiful stranger…" were befittingly blasting over his stereo. As I hopped in, he yelled to me over the music that I shouldn't be hitch hiking alone.

"Really? I disagree under the circumstances," I yelled back singing loudly and moving along to the lyrics "To know you, Is to love you, You're everywhere I go, And everybody knows…."[17] We looked into each other's eyes and started laughing at the utter absurdity of just how apropos the moment was with two beautiful

[17] Madonna, "Beautiful Stranger," Track #1 on *Music from The Motion Picture Austin Powers "The Spy Who Shagged Me,"* Maverick- Warner Bros., 1999, CD

strangers. I marveled at this unplanned perfection, and the fact that I was back in the free flow once again.

When I noticed my flight to Ecuador had a layover in Costa Rica, I saw an unexpected opportunity to finally visit the country I had set my sights on years ago. Despite my father's warning that it wouldn't be possible without paying change fees, I managed to arrange a one month layover free of charge. My first night in downtown San Jose, I met a young group of Ticos at the Vishnu Vegetarian Restaurant. Before long, they had convinced me to attend the biggest music festival of the year with them at Las Palmas the following night. We spent over an hour waiting in a line that wound down half a city block for public transportation to the event. Once there, the high energy was contagious. It was a huge lawn concert, and everyone knew the songs, singing along in Spanish as they threw their hands up in the air or shook their beers up high. We stayed until one in the morning, but then waited even longer for a bus back to the city. By the time we boarded, it was 3:00 a.m. My chaperone, the young black Tico that had been hitting on me all night, let me have one butt cheek on the bus seat, and he sat on the floor in the aisle, falling asleep while hugging his knees to his chest. I on the other hand, even with half a seat, was too afraid I'd fall over. I rested my head on the seat in front of me and watched him twitch and jump recounting the events of the day. Even though I was thoroughly exhausted, I was so thankful that they had invited me with open hearts to share this part of their culture.

When I left San Jose, I went directly to Puerto Viejo on the Caribbean side of Costa Rica, which was against the advice of my new Tico friends. They warned me about the Rastas, the weed and to be careful alone at the reggae nights. This sounded like exactly what I was interested in, so after recovering from Las Palmas, I made my way there. Shortly after arriving, I befriended a group of cute surfer dudes from San Diego, California. I narrowed my focus on one in particular who was a classic looking tanned, blue eyed, bleached blonde with a warm, carefree smile. He invited me to join him and his friends on a magic mushroom trip in Manzanillo. I had already rented a bike and a snorkel to explore out that way on my own, having a magical experience sober. I encountered howler monkeys, a sloth and one of the most beautiful beaches I had ever seen at Punta Uva. I shared my "local knowledge" with them, being a bit of a show off trying to earn some respect and gain hook-up headway.

Feeling the mushrooms coming on, we began to get giggly as we walked the trail, and soon, we arrived at the shore break with some large rocks. I insisted I would like to swim there, so they gave me a pair of goggles, and I proceeded to show them just what a cool chick I was. I headed out to swim around the rocks all by myself and they continued on their hike, leaving me alone in the ocean. I saw a few fish doing the same thing I was trying to do, avoid getting slammed into the rocks with the surf perpetually breaking. Before I knew it, I was caught in a riptide. I was trying to swim back towards the shore but making no progress. With the waves crashing into the rocks, and all around me, I began to take on water. Between coughing and belching up water, I gasped for air, and true panic and fear set in. I would sink, then cough and then fight again, but I began tiring. I tried to swim froggie style, my strongest stroke, but it was starting to feel hopeless.

As I floated there, face down, I heard the gentle sound of drumming and angelic voices singing. My girlfriend Cassie who had died recently in a car accident was there, her fluid spirit drifting near me amongst countless other loving beings. A warm white light surrounded us that came from a brighter, center point in the distance. This light blanketed and connected us in pure, unconditional love. I sensed the source of the light was God or Love, which was orchestrating *everything* not only on this angelic plane, but it was the governing force everywhere, throughout all dimensions. I felt total peace. Everyone was free. Everyone was equal. Cassie reassured me that I was safe and welcomed me to stay in this state eternally. I knew that I could hold my breath forever and never have to worry about anything again; no bills, no taxes, no shoulds, no schedules or stress. Just complete loving perfection, peace and bliss. This was my moment. If I wanted to stay in the ultimate altered state, possibly for an eternity, then here was a solid invitation.

I lifted my head and looked back at the coconut palms on the shore, which made me think of earthly pleasures. I thought of all the other coasts on other continents; Africa and Europe, the places I still wanted to see in this lifetime. I knew these places didn't matter on the other side, that you could see everything, know everything, and be at one with absolutely no desire. I also knew my life in this body and with this family was an opportunity. It was a gift. I thought of my parents and how devastated they would be if I were to drown in Costa Rica on magic mushrooms. I'm not sure if it was the desire to see and do more in this lifetime, to not hurt my family, or not giving my father the opportunity to say, "I told her so," about all my wild adventures. It was probably a combination of all of these things that, as tempting as it was to stay in the afterworld, were confirmation that I still wanted to live.

I remembered what I was taught to do if you're caught in a riptide and started with relaxing. I gasped at the surface and floated there on my back, wondering if rip currents can pull you under. I rested and prepared myself to hold my breath in the event that this were to happen, thinking I would pop out eventually somewhere else. I could still hear the sound of soft drumming. I felt the body high of the mushrooms and the bright white light, now of the Caribbean sunshine on my face and my skin. I was acutely aware that I could hold my breath and drift into oneness forever. After resting for some time, I felt I had regained enough strength to attempt swimming back to shore. As I swam at a different angle, truly exhausted, something in the tide had shifted. As I got closer, the waves actually gently pushed me in. When I reached the beach, the boys were waiting there, concerned. I tried to keep my cool and didn't tell them all the details at once. "I saw a few fish and got caught in a rip current, but eventually I remembered what to do."

I spent the days that followed *consumed* by this experience, replaying it over and over again in my head. It really was the ultimate spiritual experience, and in it, there was so much insight about our psyches, life, death, the afterlife, and spiritual immortality. I began to see a huge cross-over between death and psychedelics. I had thought for some time that psychoactive substances bring your subconscious thoughts to the forefront of your mind. This is why I didn't worry about having a bad trip or "never coming back" because I knew there wasn't a whole lot of darkness dwelling in the corners of my mind. Life was unicorns and rainbows for me, and that was clearly reflected in every psychedelic journey I took. The people that I knew who had challenging trips were people who had experienced a lot of loss, trauma, fear, or self-doubt in their lives. I surmised that these substances have the ability to magnify our psyches, bringing whatever lies beneath the surface to the foreground of our minds.

Now I began to ask myself if what we experience as we transition to the afterlife is also a representation of our subconscious minds. *Are our brains releasing a lifetime of programming when we die?* There are so many accounts of NDEs where the person who dies experiences something which supports his/her personal belief system. Reported NDEs include (but are certainly not limited to) devout Catholics seeing Mother Mary, Muslims having the Angel of Death appear, and Christians meeting God. If we have held deeply rooted beliefs regarding purpose and creation our whole life, why wouldn't there be potential for our psyche to release the images of our individual truth as we transition to the afterlife?

Yogic philosophy derived its teaching of the afterlife from the Vedic texts (Upanishads) which describe humans as having three bodies: the physical (or gross) body; the subtle (or astral) body, which includes our feelings, senses, knowledge, intellect, the subconscious and the ego; and then the causal (or bliss) body, which is essentially our soul that contains all of our previous experiences and memories from this lifetime, and all of our past lives. This text states that when we die, both our subtle and our causal bodies leave the physical body together. If this is true, as we shed our physical identity, we are actually taking our memories *and* what we carry in our intellect and subconscious mind (including our sense of God, Jah, Allah, the Divine, white light, pure consciousness, or whatever we hold to be true). My experience of hearing drums, seeing a friend who had recently passed, and the white light of unconditional love was definitely a direct reflection of my own hippie drum circle peace and love belief system.

Oddly, after this event I did not feel extremely lucky to be alive, but to the contrary, I was experiencing a deep sense of loss having chosen to stay here on Earth. I shared my NDE and this feeling of existential depression with the few people I had become close with in Puerto Viejo. They listened well, but no one could really relate having never experienced something like this themselves. I continued journaling, theorizing and struggling to "integrate," or apply something tangible that I had extracted from the experience into my everyday life. At that time, no one I knew was familiar with the concept of integration, which is a spiritual buzzword today. I didn't know how I could live in both the spiritual and the material world simultaneously, and I realized that had *always* been my struggle. In the past, living a spiritual life had meant staying in the bliss of peace and love, completely renouncing the material world. It was either throw my wallet into the forest or work some kind of unfulfilling cubicle desk job. There was nothing in between. It would be nearly two decades before I'd hear Alan Watts' talk about the importance of grounding ourselves and learning to, "handle the game of ordinary human existence and play by ordinary human rules."[18]

After sulking, writing and processing for multiple days, I decided that if I was going to remain here on the physical plane, I needed to come down out of the clouds and find a way to be in the material world for a while. I felt if I was going to move forward, I needed to stop brooding and start living again. I made a conscious effort to press pause on all my processing and temporarily push this experience out of my mind. I vowed to focus more on the tangible beautiful natural surroundings and the massage job I had landed at a party hostel.

TT at Rocking T's Hostel had a massage table with overhead bars built for me on the beach, and I had been receiving work there periodically. I had a free place to stay in an old school bus that was parked at a Dutch owned lodge, so I extended my layover another month. When my parents heard this, they began planning a trip to Costa Rica to visit me. I started to settle back into the material plane; riding my bike to town, working and visiting the local beaches. I made new friends and enjoyed live music at nights, crushing on an Italian saxophone player. I hired a Spanish tutor and spent my free time amongst the toucans, monkeys and sloths. I decided to go to Savit, a spiritual retreat center, before my parents' visit to resume my processing and hopefully find a bit more clarity there.

One of my best friends in Alaska had spent time at Savit's main Ashram in Pune, India, which is what inspired me to move in this

---

[18] Lecture by Alan Watts entitled "The Secret of LSD & How to Handle it"

direction. I was interested in taking part in the daily meditations and ecstatic dance classes she had told me about. Upon arrival, any hopes I had of integrating my NDE by sharing in some talk therapy with these folks were quickly dashed. Nearly every ultra-spiritual person I met there had the same mantra, "Too bad you're only here for just one week." I understood that was a short stint in contrast to their longggg annual stays of two or three months. "Too bad you won't meet Farhan," (their guru) was another common remark, as well a list of other ceremonies and activities that I would not be participating in. Part of me knew this collective expression was because they wanted me to experience more of the juicier things the place had to offer (like ayahuasca ceremonies and silent meditation retreats), but after hearing it multiple times, it became negative and redundant. I mostly felt relieved that Farhan wasn't present, as guru mentality made me slightly uncomfortable. I didn't doubt his state of enlightenment or teachings, and it would have been nice to do a month of silence with him there, but it would have been even nicer if I had felt more loving acceptance during that week. I devoted four hours of my day to cooking or cleaning to stay in very basic open-air accommodations for a reasonable rate. I attended all the yoga classes and active meditations they were offering, and I actually did find more spiritual clarity. It just wasn't in the form I had expected.

Later, a friend of mine who spends her winters in Sedona, Arizona near a Savit Meditation Center summed it up by comically calling these people Savit Snobs. For me, the idiosyncrasies of this particular branch of hippism magnified the counterculture at large. As the same questions and conversations kept coming up, the judgement of this spiritual community became very apparent. They were trying to see where my piece fit into their puzzle. As far as I could tell, acceptance and ranking factors mainly included, but were not limited to: my knowledge of permaculture, if I'd been to Pune, India, and how much time I had spent with Farhan. The disapproval on their faces was obvious as I admitted I had never built composting toilets or done an enema cleanse before. They were perplexed as to why I was there because even though I still dressed naturally and didn't wear any makeup, I wasn't adorned with crystals or tie-dyes, and I no longer had my dreads. Without these cultural signals, they couldn't lump me into their same box, which even though is "outside of the box" of mainstream thinking, I saw now, was a dogma of its own and one that I no longer felt the need to be part of.

These people were way too cosmic for me. And although they had rainbow chakra ego auras, it was still *ego*. They were throwing around their spiritual lingo and "processing" everything that came their way. It's great to want to take personal responsibility and strive to be a better person, but I realized just how tired I had become of analyzing everything, especially now that I was being analyzed. *What happened to just accepting and loving yourself and others in the present moment? How is advertising the extent of your alternativeness or spirituality and the desire to climb up or fit within the hippie hierarchy any different than climbing the corporate ladder?* It's not. It's the same energy of wanting to be accepted and achieve status by looking outside of ourselves for happiness and validation. A light went on. *There is no need to search or look to exterior factors to establish our identity if we are already found.*

I thought back to my NDE, to that feeling of unconditional love and the fact that each angelic being was blanketed in and connected to that white light. I had been shown that we are all a continuation of unconditional love or God's light. We are each unique expressions of the Divine and can choose to be any form of that expression: farmers, anarchists, evangelists, doctors, artists, politicians, whatever. And *that* is how I could integrate all of this; by trying my best to honor each individual that is sent my way because we are all an expression of the Divine. We are all essentially God.

I met a few radiant people there who embodied this, but for the most part, these devotees were holier than thou, and the more they talked about their chakras, the guru, or their "beloved," the more disenchanted I became. Maybe it took fully immersing myself in this for me to realize that ten minute tantric hugs just aren't my thing, and I definitely wasn't basing my life on the Mayan calendar. I was beginning to understand that I *was* more grounded in physical reality than I had previously thought, and that I didn't want to talk about energy, auras or my feelings all day long. I had already been transmuting all of these esoterisms into my physical existence through my free-spirited nature as lightness, with laughter, and an underlying feeling of joy and wonder. Surprisingly, by coming here, I had grounded into a stronger sense of who I am and the fact that unconditional love and doing what I love unconditionally had always been a huge part of being me. By the time I went to San Jose to meet my parents, I was feeling more relaxed and self-assured, excited to be in Costa Rica with them.

Chapter 22

Atonement

The feeling of relaxation I had leaving Savit quickly unraveled as both my mom and I gasped, tightened our bodies, and held onto the oh-shit handles while my dad drove their rental car on the wrong side of the narrow winding roads. And comment we did, which did not change his driving, but instead evoked a snappy response that it absolutely *was* necessary to drive like a maniac (our words) to avoid the potholes. His final question, which mostly shut us up being, "Does one of *you* want to drive?" And so there we were. As Ram Dass famously said, "If you think you're enlightened, go spend a week with your family."

Despite my dad's driving and a whole lot of rain, we did have a great week together. We stayed right on Punta Uva beach, which I would have never splurged on had I been on my own. My parents chatted with the French ex-pat owners and their talking green parrots, which my dad got a huge kick out of. I took them to see where I was working at Rocking T's and introduced them to TT the owner and infamous pot smoking gigolo. As a joint was being passed around a small circle, my mom in all seriousness asked him, "What's the policy around marijuana here?" TT responded with, "Light it if you've got it," half coughing, half holding his breath in, as he hit the roach. My father chuckled, and I had a yesssss moment, doing a little internal anti-establishment dance. He offered some to me, but I shook my head no, taking that as a cue to show them around. I began a tour of the property which was slowly getting covered in mosaic art work by collaborating guests. I showed them the shared bathrooms, community kitchen, lockers and the hammock zone. As we proceeded to walk to the beach, my mom marveled at how ingenious TT's concept was and what a shame it was that in America we didn't have more hostels like in Europe. "Look at how smart he is having his guests do all that artwork and it makes it so cool." *Yep*, I smiled as I thought *this is what a business in an alternative reality looks like.*

One evening while we were out to eat, a Belgian friend Jasper sidled up next to me, giving me a hug and unexpectedly joining us for dinner. I introduced my parents and they promptly asked Jasper what he did, meaning for work. He described the yoga retreat center where he worked as a vegan chef and welcomed them to come visit, mentioning I had been there before. My dad continued to gather more information. "How far is it? It's not *on* the beach? *Why* would anybody go there? Does it have a pool?" Jasper laughed as he explained that most of their guests go there to disconnect from the rest of the world and are happy to be in nature where the views of the ocean are amazing. Also, he confirmed, "No, there is no pool." He added his own opinion saying he didn't understand why anyone had pools at all. "The ocean is my pool."

I admired the way he was able to laugh off my father's questioning and opinions, not seeming to take anything to heart. I noticed a healthy distance that I now felt between my parents and myself. It was the knowledge that we were connected, yes, but separate, and they were in no way a representation of me, or I of them. I no longer felt that familiar twinge of embarrassment for anything they said or did that went against counterculture protocol. My father went on to agree, "I can understand that," he said regarding Jasper's point that most pools are not eco-friendly, using chemicals and an incredible amount of energy for a luxury item people rarely used. My eyes glazed over, and I became lost in thought as my dad launched into a conversation about the chemistry of saltwater pools.

As pool owning people, they didn't see Jasper's viewpoint as a personal attack either, but just as an opinion. Likewise, my rebellion was never a direct assault against my parents, nor was it a reflection of *them* or their parenting in any way. It was *my* quest for freedom and self-discovery outside of the system; a system they had built their whole identity around, finding a sense of worth in those structures. So of course they took my flat-out refusal to get with their program personally, exactly how I had translated Riley's disbelief in massage therapy, or my parents' disapproval of my radical lifestyle to mean they didn't believe in me. I was beginning to see that just as my parents' had attached their self-worth to social/ economic factors, I had attached my identity to exterior things as well: yoga, meditation, massage therapy, and free-spirited travel. I understood that just as we are not our physical bodies, we are not these *things* either, and that we *could* love and care about one another on a deeper level, regardless of the exterior aspects we have chosen to identify with in our lives. Their love for me had probably never wavered even amidst their disapproval, as I had assumed it did. They had continued to be there for me throughout my journey, offering their support, visiting me in Alaska, putting me through massage school, and now being here with me in Costa Rica.

As I sat there and listened to Jasper explain his seasonal job and his lifestyle, I didn't really care if they understood it. It would be nice if my life choices were somehow being validated by other people's stories, but it was no longer necessary. I had found *my* definition of success; a way to live out my own unique expression of the Divine, doing what makes me truly happy, outside of the limitations of society. As I embraced what it is to be me, gratitude came rushing in for my "normal childhood," which in the past, running with misfits, I had also been embarrassed of. The stability that my parents provided me with growing up, and their belief in me when I was younger that I could be anything (which in their eyes was a doctor, a lawyer, the president), was what had nourished my optimism and commitment to focus on the positive. I never doubted and always accepted things as they came, so in this way, things always worked out for me, no matter what the outcome. I carried with me the practicality of both my parents. I am my mother's daughter; empathic and artistic with a strong sense of community. I got my stupid sense of humor, love for travel and the great outdoors from my dad. I have his same curiosity and skepticism (which often times he aims at me), that I've used to question social norms and collective belief systems.

Of course, we continued to have a human experience together being challenged by *my* low blood sugar, general disagreements and the rain. But overall, things felt good. Once my parents left, I extended my layover one more month (still free of charge), maximizing my ninety day stay in Costa Rica. After that, I'd shove off to Ecuador on my own, with absolutely *zero* plans, and no guidebook, to be completely open to what life would bring. Because, well, that's just how I roll, and that's the unconventional essence of being me! I was beginning to acknowledge just how messy my journey had been. There was a lot of unlearning and misunderstanding that had taken place. There were lessons learned, and then at times, forgotten again. I knew I didn't have everything figured out. That no one does, and I preferred to stay that way, in a state of wonder and *unknowing*. I was thankful that I had the courage to go against the social current to try to forge my own way in the world. In fact, I've become convinced that if more people would step out and allow themselves to be guided by the things they love and truly believe in, then the state of the world would absolutely, positively change. I've also come to accept that this is my magic and these are my super powers; my ability to let go of expectations, to accept what is, to move into the unknown heart first, to trust my intuition and remain open to any and all possibilities. But above all else, I've discovered that the real super power in this world is to hold the intention to try my (*our*) best to receive everyone and every situation in the highest vibration which is LOVE.

A Special Thanks...

To my parents who continued to show me love throughout my entire journey which was truly heart wrenching for them at times. To my husband Mike (whose character you will meet in the next book) who has always been unconditionally supportive in our relationship. To my friends who acted as editors in the beginning: Laura, Erik, and Patti, and my sister Amy who helped me immensely reading *Heart First* at least three times before it was published. A big thanks to my niece Kelly, who *really* lit my fire in the beginning and helped me to get *Heart First's* socials and website off the ground. To Amy Kochek (my editor) for all her coaching, experience, and encouragement. Amy Pescod for my logo and cover art. Denise Barringer for her cover design and amazing graphics. To all my friends who consistently asked me how my book was coming, FOR YEARS, always believing in me. To the characters in the book, those friends and acquaintances (some of which I have completely lost contact with) who helped to influence and shape my journey. To you dear readers for your love, support and interest. But above all... I thank God, Jah, The Universe, Mother Earth, Father Sky- that loving force that continues to teach, guide and provide for all of us!

Made in the USA
Coppell, TX
01 October 2021